WOMEN
OF
VICTORIAN
HASTINGS
1830-1870

**THE LIVES & OCCUPATIONS OF WOMEN
IN HASTINGS & ST LEONARDS
IN THE MID-19TH CENTURY**

HELENA WOJTCZAK

Published by
THE HASTINGS PRESS
PO Box 96 Hastings TN34 1GQ
hastings.press@virgin.net
www. hastingspress.co.uk

forthcoming, by the same author:
Notable Women of Victorian Hastings - ISBN 1 904 109 00 4
Down & Out in Victorian Hastings - ISBN 1 904 109 01 2

Set in Times New Roman 10 bold

Cover the Bloomer costume (see page 20), probably never worn in Hastings, from the
song-sheet Mrs. Bloomer's Own, 1850s. Enthoven Collection, Victoria & Albert
Museum. Cover design by the author.

Printed and bound by Antony Rowe Ltd, Eastbourne

ABOUT THE AUTHOR

Helena Wojtczak BSc (Hons) was born in Sussex and raised in London. She has
worked on the railways, in administration and as a musicians' agent. After
graduating in psychology she undertook three years' postgraduate study in
social, women's, and oral history. As Consultant Historian to the National
Railway Museum, York, she co-produced a major exhibition on railway workers
in 1996-7. In 1998 St Mary-in-the-Castle Arts Centre, Hastings, displayed her
work on the suffrage movement, and in 2002 she produced an exhibition on
Victorian Women of Hastings for Hastings Museum. Helena has produced two
award-winning history websites: Railway Women in Wartime and Women of
Hastings & St Leonards and has contributed to several others including The
Victorian Web and Encyclopedia Titanica. She has been featured in newspapers
and has appeared on television and radio, and has been published by the Oxford
University Press and by the Railway Ancestors Family History Society. Helena
currently lives in St Leonards and is writing a book on railway labour history.

CONTENTS

In loving memory

of

Teresa Cieslak Wojtczak

1949~2001

Preface

Women of Victorian Hastings 1830 ~1870 is the first work ever published on the subject. It focuses mainly on the lives of everyday women in an ordinary seaside town, with special regard to how they earned their living. It belongs to the genre of neighbourhood, community and town history as well as that of working people and of women. The current upsurge in interest in these areas is most heartening, since there are many stories to be told of the great majority of the population who, being neither royalty, aristocracy or military, have been neglected in conventional histories. This book is my contribution towards that area of research. Its forthcoming companion, *Notable Women of Victorian Hastings,* is a volume of short biographies of some outstanding women connected with Hastings, together with an annotated list of some interesting female visitors. These books began life as private research projects, prompted by personal interest, which were developed by the late Julian Rhodes into a website before being greatly expanded and published as books.

My thanks are due to the staff of Hastings Reference Library and Hastings Museums, to Denise for technical support, and to Cameron Moffett for her many helpful suggestions.

Helena Wojtczak
St Leonards-on-Sea, April 2002

A young, fashionable lady and an elderly widow; just two of the many faces of mid-19th century womanhood.

A Brief Note About
Hastings & St Leonards

Hastings is an ancient fishing town whose centre was in the Bourne Valley, between the East and West hills. From about 1760 it gained favour as a watering place for the well-to-do and its popularity grew after physicians endorsed sea-water as a cure for most ills. By the 1830s demand for lodgings had outstripped supply. This, together with the housing needs of the growing population, propelled the spread of Hastings westwards into the Priory Valley. In 1828 architect James Burton founded St Leonards, a purpose-built resort one mile to the west of Hastings. Both towns grew and prospered: between 1801 and 1851 the population increased from 3,000 to 17,000 and they were described as two of the most beautiful watering-places in Britain.

The arrival of the railway in 1846 greatly expanded the towns' tourism: the journey time from London was reduced from eight hours to three. Hastings station, opened in 1851, was sited in the Priory Valley where, over the next fifteen years, the post office and banks relocated, and new hotels and churches were built. This shifted the centre of Hastings to the Priory Valley, and the Bourne Valley became known as the Old Town.

Looking east across the rooftops of Robertson Street to the Castle from St Michael's Mount, now Prospect Place, c1861.

Introduction

The history of men has been palmed off on us as universal history.

Deirdre Beddoes, Professor of History.

History books specifically about women exist mainly to rectify the omissions of other works. The history of women is not adequately covered by books that focus on men because, until the late 20th century, women were subject to special laws and social customs which governed every part of their lives. Our knowledge of women's past has been obscured by standard history books. Male names are routinely selected as examples in secondary sources and when the information is re-worked they are cited again. If women are mentioned a brief account is given about some of note - or notoriety - then the narrative swiftly reverts to reciting only the deeds of men.

Because history text-books focus on MPs, mayors, councillors, huge landowners and large businesses, few women feature. Omitting to explain that women were straight-jacketed at every turn by legal disabilities and man-made social structures invites readers to misinterpret women's absence from civic life and professions as voluntary. Furthermore, when historians mention 'the worker', 'the shopkeeper', 'the philanthropist' or 'the publican', they habitually cite men as examples. One's mind becomes so saturated with men's names, by the constant repetition of 'he', 'his' and 'him', that the reader is duped into believing that no women existed in those categories. It is, therefore, necessary to redress the balance by writing specifically about women.

The hidden majority

Despite their near-absence from many written histories, since records began women were - and still are - in the majority. In 1851, women outnumbered men nationally by half a million. The population of Hastings was then 17,621, of whom over 55% were female, and ten years later this had risen to 58%: there were 3,859 more females than males. In some parishes, almost two-thirds of the population was female.[1] These parishes were in the newly-built areas of central Hastings and St Leonards, which attracted many wealthy visitors and immigrants from London and elsewhere, who employed a large number of female servants. In the district encompassing Marina, Caves Road, West Ascent and Gloucester Lodge, St Leonards, there were 554 males to 1098 females - and that included two boys' boarding schools, which bolstered the number of males. Similarly, two sets of double-villas called Upland Views and The Lawn, built in the 1850s overlooking the St Leonards Subscription Gardens were, from the outset, inhabited almost exclusively by women. Fifteen years later the 1871 Census shows that 90% of the inhabitants were female. Women headed 14 of the 16 households, which typically comprised an elderly widow or spinster, some female

relations and numerous female servants. In 1871 women comprised 80% of the residents of Wellington Square.[2]

While the archetypal 'worker' is presumed to be male, in some areas more women than men were employed. In Church Road, St Leonards, a new road of middle-class villas, 61 women and 20 men were employed.[3] In the commercial district of central Hastings, in St Mary-in-the-Castle ward, there were 831 females to 462 males in 1861. To give but one of many examples, the owner of a millinery shop at 4 Castle Street was the sole male in a household of 14, comprising his wife, five milliners, two saleswomen, two dressmakers, a mantle-maker, a cook and a housemaid.

The reasons for this imbalance were manifold. James Burton built St Leonards for the wealthy, who employed many domestic servants: in most cases, the servants outnumbered the family. About 95% of domestic servants were female. Hastings new town and, most especially St Leonards, attracted rich spinsters and widows to settle in the area, where large, new houses awaited them, many of which had open aspects to the sea, which was reputed to have health-giving properties. Women with a private income, or with money to invest in rental properties could find no finer place in which to reside. In addition, abundant opportunities for charity work existed, owing to the grinding poverty in the Old Town. Another factor was the large number of schools, seminaries and convalescent homes, all of which sprung up as a result of the reputedly healthy sea air and the new, large buildings. These establishments were run by female proprietors, nurses, orderlies, matrons, schoolmistresses and servants.

The numerical superiority of women was obvious to any casual observer for the streets were busy with shop-girls and housemaids on errands, women served in most shops and the churches were full of women. It was a standing joke among residents and visitors, one of whom remarked,

> Everyone knows that St Leonards has this similarity to Paradise: "that there is neither marrying nor giving in marriage", the female population prepondering at the rate of about five to one.[4]

In contrast, the eastern parishes - the Old Town - were the working class areas. There were fewer wealthy people, and consequently fewer domestic servants, there were also fewer spinsters and more employed males than females. There were also many more children, who were born in roughly equal numbers of each sex. These areas also contained far more persons indigenous to the area. For these reasons, the sexes were more evenly balanced in the Old Town.

REFERENCES

[1] A similar situation arose in Bristol where, in one wealthy parish, St Paul's, women comprised 73% of the population in 1863.

[2] Including the *Castle Hotel*.

[3] There were 132 female and 43 male residents.

[4] *Hastings & St Leonards Chronicle,* 22 May 1874.

The Status of Women

The Victorians … made a fearful hash of the problem of woman…
Their moral dualism .. might be amusing in architecture or painting,
but it involved endless cruelty towards flesh and blood.

R. J. Cruikshank.[1]

In the 1860s one-time Hastings resident Bessie Rayner Parkes calculated that, if society were divided into 13 units, one would represent the aristocracy, three the middle ranks and nine the working masses. However, all women, whatever their class, shared a special status *as females*,[2] and suffered particular disadvantages in government, law, marriage, money, business and employment. Women and men were believed to be completely different from each other and this was reflected in every aspect of public and private life. The railways offered women-only carriages and waiting-rooms, there were separate schools for each sex, some hotels - notably the *Queen's* at Hastings - had separate coffee rooms for men and women and some churches, such as Christ Church, had separate pews for each sex. Few jobs were performed by both sexes and where they were women were paid half to two-thirds the wages of men for the same work.

Many people think that 'positive discrimination' is a modern idea; in fact Victorian men practised it with great zeal, reserving for themselves every position as MPs, town commissioners, councillors, freemen, aldermen, members of Boards of Guardians, judges, magistrates, overseers, coroners, jurors, solicitors, police officers, journalists, civil servants and clergymen. Every decision about public policy, every law and bylaw, every rule and regulation was made by men without consulting women and only men were permitted to interpret and administer the decisions of the men in power. Only men could vote for which men would govern. Entitlement to vote was, supposedly, based on property qualifications yet female landowners such as Lady Frances Elphinstone of Ore Place, a widow with 530 acres who employed 15 men, were denied the vote, while some of their own labourers were enfranchised.[3] Some progress was made in 1869, when the Municipal Reform Act gave widows and unmarried women householders the vote in municipal elections.

The economic structure hindered women from owning or inheriting wealth, throwing most into involuntary dependence upon men.[4] Fathers routinely bequeathed to sons, partly because anything inherited by a daughter would later pass to her husband.

With a Queen as Head of State, it was ironic that women lived under such total male authority. This state of affairs was not entirely the result of ancient legislation. For example, an Act of 1835 stopped unmarried women who were qualified (by property) from voting in parish-based elections (such as for Poor Law Guardians), and an Act of 1857 reaffirmed that men, but not women, could obtain a divorce solely on the grounds of adultery.

The 'Woman Question' was discussed in newspapers, magazines and journals, in parliament and at home. Woman's 'mission', her 'sphere' and her 'influence' were battlefields upon which competing ideologies strove for dominance. Some people challenged the narrow lives of women and argued for greater opportunities; others believed vehemently that women should be restricted to domestic work and child-rearing. A single issue - that of women being trained and employed as watch-makers - dominated the letters-pages of the *Hastings & St Leonards News* for several months in 1857 after a lecture on the subject was given in Hastings.

The 'cult of womanhood' preached that women should be religious and god-fearing, and pure of heart, mind and body, which entailed pre-marital chastity and marital submission without enjoyment. They were expected to live contentedly in a state of perpetual childhood, passively accepting the actions and decisions of men, to whom they were supposed to be happily subservient. Women who declined to attain this idealised stereotype were criticised, even shamed, into complying. Coventry Patmore, a one-time Hastings resident,[5] wrote a poem in the 1850s entitled *The Angel in the House*, in which he presented his submissive angel-wife as the stereotype to which all women should aspire. She was meek, humble and tranquil, and lived only to please her husband. Cassell's 3rd edition of the poem popularised it among the masses.

The Education of Girls

Prior to the introduction of state education in 1870, social class determined the type of education each child received but, in every social class and level of income, boys' education was considered of greater importance than that of girls. As late as 1871, 26 percent of brides, compared with 10 percent of bridegrooms, could not even sign their names and had instead to write an X beside their names in the parish register.

The poor learned what they needed to know for life from parents or grandparents. Some children attended a school run by an unqualified 'Dame'; these were of dubious educational worth and acted more as a crèche for the under sevens. Richer families had a resident governess until the children were old enough to attend a private seminary or boarding school. While boys learned a wide range of subjects including moral philosophy, Greek, Latin, geometry and science, girls were taught domestic and arts subjects with the intention that they would make pleasing and useful companions to men. An educated woman with opinions, who could challenge, debate and speak authoritatively was a hideous prospect for most men.

Fathers educated their sons, or apprenticed them to their own trade, and neglected their daughters, because their 'trade' was marriage. Given the numerical imbalance of the sexes not all women could marry, leading Jessie Boucherett to call the system 'wicked and cruel, and based on a fallacy.'[6] She and many other feminists argued that women should be allowed to attend training colleges and universities, but doctors claimed that women were mentally unsuited for education.

Girls were raised to obey and any signs of rebellion were swiftly crushed. It was legal for parents to beat children and Judge William Blackstone had ruled that husbands could even administer 'moderate correction' to disobedient wives; indeed, the greatest control a man could gain over another human being was by marriage.

MARRIAGE & MAIDENHOOD

The 1851 Census revealed that, of women aged 20 and over, 57% were married, 30% were spinsters and 13% were widows.

Women were indoctrinated to believe that marriage was their God-given and sole purpose in life and spinsters over 30 were pitied. Because of the enormous numerical imbalance in the sexes there were insufficient men to go around, and so not every woman could marry. Some spinsters were women left 'on the shelf' after all the available men had chosen wives but a considerable number, for various reasons, declined to marry. Of these, some were members of religious orders, while others were 'suffering' from what was then called 'sexual inversion'; that is, they were lesbians. The veil of secrecy over sexual matters in the Victorian era makes identifying them almost impossible.

Marriage will be dealt with first, because in the mid-19th century, 86% of women married at least once by the age of 50.

MARRIAGE

Under exclusively man-made laws women have been reduced to
the most abject condition of legal slavery in which it is possible
for human beings to be held ... under the arbitrary domination
of another's will, and dependent for decent treatment exclusively
on the goodness of heart of the individual master.

Dr. Fenwick Miller.[7]

The image of the Victorian lady living in an elegant house with servants obscures the reality: that she was like a bird in a gilded cage. In the mid-19th century, marriage was a form of slavery hidden under layers of hypocrisy. Promising to obey her husband was even written into every woman's marriage vows.[8] Hypocritically, men vowed 'with all my worldly goods I thee endow', but the opposite was true: upon marriage, the control of, and income from, a woman's real property, that is, property held in the form of freehold land, passed under common law to her husband, though he could not dispose of it without her consent. Her personal property, that is, money from earnings or investments, and belongings such as jewellery, passed absolutely into his control. A married woman lived under 'coverture', which meant she surrendered her legal existence on marriage: she was a *feme covert.* [9]

To prevent a woman's assets from passing automatically to her husband, a marriage settlement could be made under equity law to enable a wife to retain control over her property; however, a fiancé might not approve it. In 1849 the House of Commons received a petition which argued that marriage settlements were 'the most fertile source of domestic unhappiness', and that by 'placing her in a position of independence' they enabled a wife to 'break the vows she made at the altar': that is, the vow to obey.[10] In 1860, *The Times* declared, 'such settlements are not to be encouraged … They tend to destroy the true relation between husband and wife … The power which a woman obtains is too great'.

If she had no inheritance, a middle class woman was obliged to marry for subsistence, a condition that Hastings feminist Barbara Leigh Smith Bodichon[11] described in 1854 as 'legal prostitution'. She was alluding to a man's ownership of what was euphemistically termed 'his wife's person': this meant that wives could not withhold consent to sex.

The experience of marriage for a woman of the working classes was quite different from that of her wealthier counterparts. Not only did she have to perform all the housework herself without benefit of servants but in many cases her husband could not support her and she would have to work for wages as well, as will be seen in the next chapter.

Among some people in the poorer classes, marriage was irrelevant and cohabitation common, the woman sometimes taking the man's surname.[12] Many simply didn't share the middle-classes' belief in the necessity of marriage.

Marital strife

The marital brutality of former centuries was taboo by the Victorian era. When in 1849 a London man petitioned parliament 'to restore the ancient and venerable institutions of our ancestors, in the shape of the whipping post and the ducking stool … as a punishment for all undutiful and runaway wives'[13] no support was forthcoming. And yet a certain amount of violence by husbands was permitted, if his wife 'deserved' it, and only if he used no more force than was necessary to bring about obedience. Until 1891 if an unhappy wife escaped the police could capture her and her husband could imprison her and 'enforce his conjugal rights'.

Marital breakdown was a source of shame and embarrassment for genteel persons and separation was a last, desperate measure. Among the wealthy, estranged couples often led separate lives in their spacious homes. Well-brought-up gentlemen and ladies did not enter into public slanging matches, although mental, emotional and physical abuse occurred, it was

FILLING UP THE CENSUS PAPER

WIFE OF HIS BOSOM. 'Upon my word, Mr Peewitt!
Is this the Way you Fill up your Census? So you
call Yourself the "Head of the Family" – do you –
and me a "Female?"'

Many of the jokes in the magazine *Punch* implied, rather ironically, that
wives dominated husbands.

perhaps easier to keep private. **Among the poor, however, tempers flared
and fists flew, fuelled by alcohol, poverty and frustration. In huddled
tenements and cottages domestic violence was so common that women's
screams were routinely ignored. Although men had the physical advantage
women frequently fought back and sometimes applied to magistrates for the
man to be bound over in sureties.**

**When working class marriage broke down the couple simply lived
apart, the wife commonly 'going home to Mother'. Divorce was reserved
for the very rich as each one cost about £700 (about 14 years' wages for a
poor man) and required an Act of Parliament; indeed, only four British
women had ever achieved a divorce. From 1857, however, divorce was
made available to the middle classes.[14] A man simply had to prove his wife's
adultery but a wife had to prove other causes. From 1857 husbands lost
their right to the earnings of the wives they had deserted. This greatly
benefited women because, previously, a husband who abandoned his wife
could later reappear, take all her possessions, earnings and inheritance, and
desert again. From 1857 women could apply for a protection order to
prevent this and the first woman in the towns to do so was Jane Mathern of
2 St Margaret's Terrace, in 1859.**

MAIDENHOOD

In 1851 the Census revealed that, nationally, 43% of women over 20 enjoyed the legal status of *feme sole* – a lone female.

To deal with the numerical imbalance in the sexes, some people wanted to send husbandless women to the colonies , where many men lacked wives; indeed, in October 1848 the *Hastings & St Leonards News* published a notice urging 'surplus' women to emigrate to Australia. Later a Hastings branch of the British Ladies Female Emigration Society was founded, run by Miss Whistler.

It was acceptable and common for women to form close friendships. Which of these were of an 'intimate' nature is, of course, impossible to establish. Many women set up home with a female friend. One devoted couple in Hastings were Joanna Thwaites and Mrs. Stevens. Joanna was born in 1802, the 11th of 14 children; nonetheless her inheritance was sufficient to support her. She lived alone at 6 Meadow Cottages until she became attached to a widow, Mrs. Stevens. They lived together for 30 years, first at Croft Cottages and then at 43 High Street. The devoted pair shared a bedroom until 1891, when Mrs. Stevens became ill and the doctor advised Joanna to sleep in another room. Mrs. Stevens died and Joanna,

THE FOX AND THE GRAPES

ELDERLY SPINSTER. 'So you're going to be married, dear, are you? Well, for my part, I think nine-hundred and ninety-nine marriages out of a thousand turn out miserably; but of course every one is the best judge of their own feelings.'

heartbroken, followed her less than 30 hours later.

Religion was extremely important in the 19th century and many women took holy orders. In 1834 a nunnery opened in Hastings, which later became All Soul's Convent. In the 1850s orphans were educated here and others boarded and lodged on 'very moderate terms'. In the 1860s, the nuns' walks in the extensive grounds had to be discontinued because of repeated insults from a gang of builders working on the new houses nearby. To protect the women from this harassment the Mother Superior had a large hoarding placed against the wall.

PREGNANCY AND CHILDBEARING

'Tis the old, old story,
Told so often in vain,
For man all the freedom of passion,
For woman the ruin and pain.

Ballad. Anon.

For most women, marriage marked the beginning of a relentless succession of pregnancies. They could not withhold consent to sex, advice on contraception was illegal and its practice was considered immoral, therefore, many wives were pregnant or breast feeding from wedding day to menopause. It was quite usual for women to have six, seven or more children. The 1851 Census for Hastings shows that brewer's wife Harriet Padgen had nine, as did Isabella Ranking, the wife of a surgeon; most of hers, curiously, were born 17 months apart. Sarah Nabbs, landlady of the *Pilot Inn*, Stone Street, had at least 16. On the whole, fewer children were born to the upper classes, indicating that some educated people knew about birth control. Children were the absolute property of the husband until an Act of 1839 allowed a divorced but innocent wife custody of children up to the age of seven (raised to 16 in 1873). [15]

Babies were born at home. Poor women were attended by a local unqualified midwife or nurse; the rich were attended by a doctor. Maternal deaths in 1847 were reported as 1 in 140 but were actually much higher[16] and one in six children died before their first birthday - they comprised between 26% and 40% of all deaths, and it was common for women to lose at least one child. Mrs. Emblow, of 12 Russell Street, lost all four of her offspring in their infancy. Improvements in the conditions of childbirth began around mid-century but it took time for anaesthetics, chloroform and antiseptics to come into common use, and even longer for them to be extended to poor women.

Infant deaths were particularly prevalent among the poor and inquests revealed considerable ignorance among impoverished mothers. Babies slept in drawers and boxes in stuffy, damp rooms and it was common for the Medical Officer to attribute infant deaths to incorrect feeding. Many mothers – owing to their own ill-health - were unable to produce sufficient milk and some had no idea what to feed their babies as a substitute. In 1863, Caroline Clifden of Tivoli fed her new-born on boiled bread and sugar. When he died no prosecution entailed; the coroner simply recorded that the child died as a result of being given 'injudicious' food.[17]

Premarital sex & bastardy

Although pre-marital sex was disapproved of, premarital pregnancy was fairly common among the working classes. The couple usually married, although often the girl was sent away to give birth and the child was given up for adoption, or raised by its grandparents. Illegitimate births made up about 7% of all births in England during the mid-century. The figures for illegitimacy in Hastings were given only once: in the quarterly returns for 1875, when the rate was six in 211. Illegitimate births were rare among the upper classes, because girls were more closely watched, chaperoned, and taught to keep their distance from suitors until after the wedding.

Terminating a pregnancy was illegal but this did not stop women from trying various methods of inducing miscarriage. Hot baths and gin were reputed to work and back-street abortionists existed, although no evidence was found of any in Hastings. Kearsley's Original Widow Welch's Pills -'a safe and certain remedy in removing those obstructions' - were advertised on the front page of the *Hastings & St Leonards News*, though their efficacy must be doubted since infanticide was so common.

Unmarried mothers were in a pitiful social and financial predicament. Outcast from her family, abandoned by her seducer, facing dismissal from work and alienated from all sources of support, a single mother was usually forced to endure childbirth alone and in pain. Because children 'begotten in sin' were believed to inherit their parents' moral weakness, orphanages refused to accept bastards, although they constituted the largest number of destitute children. The editor of a Hastings newspaper commented:

> Once fallen, a woman becomes an outcast, - believed by none, cared-for by few, despised by most, and looked-upon as the fair spoil of every fellow, married or unmarried'.[18]

Employment was hard to obtain for single mothers: the child would often be placed with a wet-nurse and kept secret from employers; however, Maria Ranger, herself the offspring of an unmarried mother,[19] ran a lodging house while raising her daughter Elizabeth, who was born in 1832.

The Poor Law of 1733 stipulated that a father was responsible for the maintenance of his illegitimate child. This was later thought to encourage female immorality and sole responsibility for such children was eventually shifted onto women by the Bastardy Clause in the Poor Law of 1834. A single mother could apply to a magistrate for an affiliation order. She was required to present corroborated evidence of paternity, which the man could dispute. If she was successful the father was ordered to pay up to

2/6d a week 'child support'.[20] This was supposedly half the cost of raising the child and it did not take into account the fact that unmarried pregnancy led to a woman's dismissal from work, or the refusal of charitable societies to assisted unwed mothers.[21] Even though many single mothers were the victims of 'seduction' - a term that meant anything from a promise of marriage to rape - shame and ruin was brought upon her and, in many cases, destitution and the workhouse beckoned.

By the mid-19th century there was some semblance of sympathy towards single mothers and murmurs of disapproval were directed against the man, signifying a change in social attitudes since the beginning of the century. The first woman to be committed to the new Hastings Gaol in 1829, Sarah Martin, was serving six months for 'being delivered of a bastard child'. In contrast a man's reputation was unharmed. Surgeon and Freeman of Hastings, Charles Steven Crouch, was summonsed three times between 1801 and 1804 for siring three children by two women, and made to pay towards their maintenance. This seems not to have hindered his political career: he was eight times Mayor of Hastings and it was recorded that he was 'universally respected.'[22] It is worth noting that, as a JP, it later fell to him to hear affiliation cases brought against other men.

Affiliation cases were heard in public and frequently attracted crowds with prurient interests. When in 1860 Edward Waters, a 'tan-frock' (i.e., a fisherman), disputed fatherhood of a child born to Elizabeth Mann, the court was 'crowded with members of the fishing interest, who appeared to be highly delighted with the obscene revelations'. Waters left the court at 'boiling point' after being ordered to pay 2s a week. If a man disobeyed the court and did not pay maintenance, he was very harshly dealt with - one in 1864 received a three-month sentence - not to seek justice for women, but because magistrates were fearful of bastard children becoming dependent on the parish. In many affiliation hearings the court was cleared of females and the unfortunate woman was left surrounded by men, including the putative father and a public gallery full of men of the general public eager to hear all the sordid details for their own entertainment. In other cases women were allowed to stay and, in some, the child was brought in as well:

> The child ... was brought into court ... and, on seeing defendant began to utter a well known word, by which a paternal-parent is made conscious of the presence of his offspring, and ultimately the repetition of "Dada! Dada! Dada!" rang so loudly in the ears, not only of the defendant, but of all present ...

The magistrate awarded the mother 2s 6d a week, which 'called forth a burst of applause from the court'.[23]

Illegitimate babies were sometimes 'farmed out' to a foster-mother. This was a private financial arrangement without state involvement. In 1860, Sarah Peake sued Thomas Ransom for failure to pay her fees, which had mounted to 12s 11d, for fostering his grandchild. Magistrates dismissed the claim since there was no written agreement. Many of these babies died mysteriously. In 1855 the coroner enquired into the death of 9-week-old Mary Jane Tester Akehurst. An affiliation order had been granted just two weeks before, ordering George Tester to pay towards maintaining the child. The mother, Mary Akehurst of Marine Parade, had put her baby out to nurse with her brother's wife Sarah, who lived at Wellington Mews. Mary said, 'Either on Wednesday or Thursday last (I forget which) I saw the child and nursed it. It appeared quite well. Yesterday I saw it again and it was then dead'. Sarah Akehurst explained, 'Some food and the breast were given to it, and it was then put in its basket by the fire, with a shawl partly over it ... In the morning I found the child dead.' Surgeon David Gabb said he believed the child died from convulsions. The jury immediately returned a verdict of 'Death from convulsions.' It is interesting to note that the baby is referred to throughout as 'it' and that she was nursed at the breast by two different women. She was farmed out to Sarah when just one week old and her mother did not visit daily, despite living nearby.[24]

Deaths of illegitimate infants under 12 months of age were disproportionately - and suspiciously - high, and were not investigated too vigorously by the coroner. A bastard was likely to become dependent upon the parish and the death of one was regarded by some as a lucky escape for rate-payers. In 1864, the illegitimate infant of a servant, born on the floor at her shabby lodgings in Frances Hope's beer-shop, was found to have died of head injuries. The coroner and the jury accepted the claim that the child had 'fallen on its head during delivery' and a verdict of accidental death was returned. In 1870 the coroner merely issued a caution to a Mrs. Birt and her young daughter, even though it was obvious that they had suffocated the girl's unwanted child at birth.

In a very few cases, women had several illegitimate pregnancies. It seems likely, if the children had different fathers, that the women were prostitutes. Selina Dennard, for example, was recorded in 1866 as raising, single-handedly, eight illegitimate children. Few couples openly raised children out of wedlock. One, 39-year-old Louisa Barnett of Tivoli Road House, named her employer William Eldridge, a 52-year-old brewer and farmer, as the father of her four children.[25] Higher up the social scale, Benjamin Leigh Smith MP raised his five illegitimate children at 9 Pelham Crescent after their mother's death in 1834.[26]

Although, as we have seen, premarital and extramarital sex went against the prevailing morality, was forbidden by the Christian religion and brought a lot of trouble, shame and, often, ruin to females who indulged in it, one Hastings gentleman experienced no difficulty in persuading a long list of ladies to abet his seven year span of adultery, which was revealed to the Court of Probate and Divorce in 1872. Well-known perfumer and hairdresser Charles Septimus Ravenscroft (b.1821) was the inventor of hair gel, and his patent rotatory hair-brushing machine was exhibited at the Hastings Industrial Exhibition in 1865. But he secretly pursued 'a course of … disgusting profligacy'. Soon after his marriage in 1863 Ravenscroft, literally behind the façade of his respectable hairdresser's shop at 33 White Rock Place, now Salmon's bookshop, began a life of 'whoredom, adultery and profligacy' with clients and staff.

Soon after marrying, he began an adulterous affair with Annie Stent, this was followed by another with Miss Cox, who was described in court as 'a sufferer of *nymphomania'*. She made out a will in his favour and, shortly afterwards, she died mysteriously in Ravenscroft's house, leaving him a handsome bequest. (Later, he used this legacy to attempt to bribe witnesses not to testify against him in his divorce case.) More affairs followed. Shop assistant Miss Blackman and her fiancé witnessed Ravenscroft engaging many times in sexual intercourse with Mrs. Wood in the kitchen of his salon during 1866. An affair with Miss Noriss was followed by another with ladies' maid Julia Sharpe, with whom 'relations' took place during her brief visits to his shop while on errands for her employer. She later became his house-servant and had a daughter by him in 1867. The court heard that he gave her 'a certain illness arising from illicit intercourse.' His next liaison was with Miss Holding, resulting in a child born at Brighton in 1869. His shop assistant Miss S. Mecklereid, a Scotswoman fifteen years his junior, twice became pregnant by him, resulting in one child and one miscarriage. After his divorce, Ravenscroft and Miss Mecklereid lived together above the shop, but the 1871 Census shows no child living there.

Having enjoyed at least seven affairs resulting in four pregnancies and three illegitimate children during his seven-year marriage, Ravenscroft divorced his wife in 1870 on the grounds of her adultery with two men (simultaneously). One, a boy of 16, was ordered to pay £100 damages to Ravenscroft, as the 'injured party'.

During his years of womanising, Ravenscroft was twice summonsed in 1866 for keeping an unruly pet. The newspaper headline *The Playful Dog of White Rock*, was uncannily apt and, like Ravenscroft himself, the dog was said to have been 'a great favourite with the ladies'.

It is interesting that, despite the prevailing sexual morality and notions of prudishness amongst Victorian spinsters, Ravenscroft nevertheless managed to persuade so many to have sexual relations with him, even though he was a married man. The prosecution's explanation was that he 'exercised the most extraordinary, the most sinister influence, on every woman he came across'. It is also interesting that, despite his scandalous behaviour having been made public, Ravenscroft continued to run a successful hairdressing business until about 1885. It is unthinkable that a serial adulteress would have fared so well.

CRINOLINES & BLOOMERS

Sing a song o' Crinoline, to a tune already set;
Four and twenty barrel hoops in a sort of cabbage net.
When the hoops are on, sir, take care of your shin –
Isn't that a pretty thing to stick a lady in?

In mid-19th-century Hastings, ladies wore gowns and mantles of shimmering silk and taffeta, sumptuous velvet and intricate lace, topped and tailed with lace-trimmed bonnets, gloves, and delicate slippers. Working women wore hard-wearing boots, garments of flannel, heavy cotton and wool, white linen aprons, and plain caps. Girls wearing strong walking boots with excessively bright-coloured dresses and gaudy jewellery were immediately recognisable as prostitutes.

In the Victorian era all upper-class and middle-class women - plus those of the lower ranks with pretensions to gentility - were tightly-laced into whalebone corsets known as stays. These were hooked in the front and the tightness was adjusted by laces in the back. Stays reduced the breathing capacity of the lungs and crowded the internal organs into unnatural and often dangerous positions. Women wore voluminous and heavy, multiple layers of skirts and cumbersome starched underskirts – a minimum of six – which trailed along the ground, picking up all kinds of unsanitary matter from the streets. The outfit weighed 15 to 20 pounds and greatly impeded women's freedom of movement. It was common for women to feel breathless and faint. Working girls strove to copy, in toned-down, inexpensive versions, the attire of fashionable ladies in order to appear genteel, elegant and well-bred. The costume attracted admiring glances from men, whose attentions and consequent marriage-proposals women eagerly sought. Men found the multiplicity of underskirts intriguingly mysterious, the accentuation of the waist highly erotic, and the swooning, helpless woman very desirable.

The issue of women's clothes became a battleground upon which feminists and anti-feminists fought. Indeed, the women's rights movement was referred to as 'Bloomerism'[27] because of the Rational Dress publicised by Amelia Bloomer in the 1850s, which became almost a 'uniform' of the movement.[28] It consisted of a jacket and a knee-length skirt over Turkish-style trousers, gathered at the ankle. Gone were the corsets; women would be able to breathe, and they would also be able to take part in sport and other activities without fear of exposing their legs. The costume was greeted with horror, disdain, and squeals of hilarity and was mocked by the Hastings newspapers.

Bloomerism comes to Hastings

Abridged from the *Hastings & St Leonards News*, 12 November, 1851

The denizens of our sober town were startled out of all sense of propriety on Wednesday evening by a lecture on this most awful 'social-ism,' at the Swan Assembly Room. A Miss Atkins addressed a crowded meeting on Bloomerism, for about three-quarters of an hour, amid mingled applause and laughter.

... Miss Atkins made her appearance, attired in the new costume, and wearing a Bloomer hat jauntily placed on one side of her head, giving her, with her smiling and rather pretty face, what the ladies called a 'wicked look'. She certainly appeared in no respect at a loss for confidence - joining merrily in the laughter which many points of her lecture readily provoked.

...It would scarcely be believed (said the lecturer) by future generations, that the women of the nineteenth century crushed their ribs, destroyed their lungs, and entailed consumption on their offspring, by the custom of tight lacing! [Much applause.] We need not wonder at the absurd ambition of the Chinese ladies to pinch their feet into a baby's size, when women in England deform themselves as they do by tight-lacing.

...The inconveniences of the long dress were next reviewed. In rainy and dusty weather it was equally in the way. It was also extravagant; and therefore was a question for husbands as well as wives - for fathers as well as daughters. It was objected that the short dress and trousers were immodest. 'Is it so?' said the lecturer (putting herself into an exhibitory open-armed posture, that the dress might be fully seen by the audience, and eventually getting, by request, on the table, for still further exhibition, amid thundering peals of laughter, and cries of 'bravo' &c.) 'Is it immodest?' said Miss Atkins again - answering the question herself by shewing the superiority of the costume even in this respect.

...And then followed an energetic and woman-like appeal to woman: 'shall we, or shall we not, be allowed to judge for ourselves? Why should men dictate to us? We never dictate to them - even if they should choose to wear a half-a-chimney-pot on their head, and call it a hat!' [Loud laughter.] 'We can tell the men that we mean to do as we please. [Cheers and renewed laughter.] If the men so much admire the long dress, let them wear it a few days, and see how they would like to be enslaved by it.

... The ladies were advised next to try the dress indoors at first. After a few days' trial, she was quite sure they would have no wish to go back to the slavery of the old fashion. ... Let women be resolved on a reform - regardless of surrounding scorn and derision.

... The prevailing feature of the entertainment was one of comicality, the really intellectual or useful being quite secondary. It was, in fact, rather a performance than a lecture; and the audience departed much refreshed by that natural medicine, which 'shakes the hypochondria from one's ribs, and the cobwebs from one's brains' - videlicet, good hearty laughter.

After Rational Dress was laughed into obscurity, in 1857 the French crinoline - a lightweight, hooped cage of flexible steel or whalebone - burst onto the fashion scene. Its size reflected social status - the most chic were 7ft in diameter. It replaced the layers of petticoats and, as the wide skirt made the waist appear small, corsets could be loosened. However, the crinoline prevented any sudden movement and was unmanageable and even humiliating. When sitting down, it sprung up wildly at the front; when walking, a gust of wind would reveal all, so in windy weather a cape was necessary to weigh it down.

In Hastings, as everywhere, there were dozens of accidents caused by crinolines, some trivial; others tragic. In Waterloo Passage in 1862, ten year old Julia Brazier died from burns after her skirt, extended by a crinoline, touched an open fire while she was tying her brother's bootlaces.[29]

By the end of the 1860s, nine million crinolines were in use. Once they spread to the masses they lost prestige, and fashionable women adopted the bustle, a steel cage attached just above the hips and fastened around the waist. By the 1870s this had been extended to just above the back of the knees and at the height of its popularity, it was horizontal. Once again corsets became excessively tight and petticoats multiplied, while skirts became longer at the back to form a small train. Women were back where they had started.

Contemporary drawing from *Punch* magazine showing in cross-section detail the construction of the 1860s French hoop crinoline.

REFERENCES

[1] Cruikshank, R. J. (1949) *Charles Dickens and Early Victorian England*, London. p149.

[2] It could be contended that women had no class on their own account, but derived it from fathers and husbands.

[3] 1836 *Register of Electors*, PNB Publications, 1990. Mrs. Bird and Elizabeth Foster were in a similar situation.

[4] Owing to loopholes in the system, a small percentage of women did inherit wealth.

[5] He rented The Mansion from 1875 until 1891 and commissioned St Mary Star of the Sea Church as a memorial to his second wife.

[6] *English Woman's Journal*, November 1862.

[7] Dr. Florence Fenwick Miller (1854-1935) one of the first women physicians. Speech at the National Liberal Club, 1890.

[8] Only since the late 20th century could women omit that promise from their wedding vows.

[9] Anglo-Norman: *feme*, woman + Old French *covert*, cover.

[10] *Shrewsbury Chronicle* 3 August 1849.

[11] See Wojtczak, H. (2002) *Notable Women of Victorian Hastings*. The Hastings Press.

[12] In a child-neglect case at Heathfield, all three couples who were witnesses were all raising families out of wedlock.

[13] *Shrewsbury Chronicle*, 3 August 1849.

[14] The poor had to wait until the Matrimonial Causes Act of 1878, which allowed a less costly judicial separation but without the right of remarriage.

[15] The Infants Custody Act of 1886 made the welfare of children the determining factor in deciding questions of custody, but even then the father remained during his lifetime the sole legal guardian.

[16] Smith, F. B. (1979) *The People's Health* 1830-1910, pp13-15, 28-31, 55-58

[17] *Hastings & St Leonards News* 1 January 1864.

[18] *Hastings & St Leonards News,* 27 April 1855

[19] Born April 1801 at Crowhurst, where half the births that year were illegitimate. (source: Parish Records.)

[20] Unless he was in the army or navy.

[21] The first charitable homes for unmarried mothers appeared in the 1880s.

[22] Courts, Sessions, and Hundreds. Hastings Museum Collection.

[23] *Hastings & St Leonards News* 25 February 1863.

[24] Coroner's Inquest, *Hastings & St Leonards News*, 9 February, 1855. A Mary Akehurst was a lodging-house keeper at 12 Marine Parade in 1864.

[25] 1851 Census.

[26] One of these children became a famous arctic explorer; another was a well-known feminist activist. See Wojtczak, H. (2002) *Notable Women of Victorian Hastings*. The Hastings Press.

[27] The term 'feminist' was not used until the 1890s.

[28] Invented in 1851 by an American, Elizabeth Miller.

[29] *Hastings & St Leonards News* 26 September 1862.

TO WEARERS OF CRINOLINE.

SIR,—Allow me to call the attention of some of your readers to the inconvenience and danger of the above article, in proof of which I beg to state the following :— Being lame, I am compelled to walk with a stick ; and while passing through one of your streets the other day, I met several ladies, and before I could move out of their way, the crinoline of one came with such violence that it forced my stick from under me, and it was with some difficulty that I saved myself from falling on the pavement. This is the second narrow escape I have had within a week from those formidable crinolines. To avoid any further collision, I am sorry to say I can see no other alternative than to keep quite out of the way of the fair sex, which would indeed be a great privation to a nervous individual like myself.

By inserting the above, you will greatly oblige, and be doing a public service.

I am, sir,

Hastings, January 12, 1860.   A VISITOR.

The various dangers and annoyances associated with wearing crinolines were publicised in the correspondence columns of Hastings' newspapers.

ANOTHER CRINOLINE ADVENTURE.— A rather laughable circumstance was enacted near the General Post Office a few days ago. A lady crossing the roadway allowed a horse and vehicle to approach close to her unheard. In attempting to retreat the lady's expansive garments swayed against the horse's leg. Just at the moment the animal lifted its foot, and it came down *crash* through the dress and— something else ; the lady's efforts to escape only causing the fluttering garments to be impaled round the pedal organ of the quadruped. Our fair friend was completely "in custody," and nothing remained for her but to keep pace with the horse until the driver could stop it and release her. Of course the occurrence was but the work of a moment, but the lady's feelings upon being set at liberty must be left to the readers' imagination.

Occupations of women in Hastings & St Leonards 1830-1870
Part 1

apple shop keeper
artist
artists' repository keeper
author
baby linen dealer
baker
bathing machine proprietor
bather
baths manager
baths proprietor
beer-shop keeper
Berlin wool dealer
blacksmith & shoeing
boarding-house keeper
bookseller
bootbinder
broker
butcher
cabinet maker
carrier
chair bottomer
chair caner
chair maker
china & glass dealer
cloakmaker
clothier
coal merchant
coffee house keeper
companion
confectioner
cook
corset maker
cow keeper
curative mesmerist
currier
dairywoman
domestic servant
drapers
dressmaker
earthenware dealer
eating house keeper
egg merchant
embroiderer
fancy repository keeper
farmer

feather dresser
fish carrier
fish hawker
fishmonger
fish seller
flower seller
fruiterer
furniture dealer
furrier
fly proprietor
general dealer
governess, private
governess, infant school
greengrocer
grocer
hairdresser
hatter
hotel keeper
hosier
ironer
ironmonger
juvenile warehouse proprietor
kitchenmaid
labourer
lacemaker
lace runner maker
lady
lady's maid
laundress
laundry maid
laundry proprietor
library proprietor
lodging-house keeper
manglewoman
mantlemaker
marine store owner
matron, gaol
matron, industrial school
matron, infirmary
matron, workhouse
milk vendor
milliner
needlewoman
newsagent
novelist

Occupations

Women want work both for the health of their minds and bodies. They want it often because they must eat and because they have children and others dependent on them – *for all the reasons that men want work.*

Barbara Bodichon, 1857

The economical position of women is one of those subjects on which there exists a 'conspiracy of silence.' While most people, perhaps, imagine that nearly all women marry and are supported by their husbands, those who know better how women live, or die, have rarely anything to say on the subject.

Josephine Butler, 1868.

In the mid-19th century, profitable and interesting employment for Britain's 3.1 million working women did not exist. Women's work was low status and almost invariably without promotion, authority, pension or security. It was taboo for well-educated girls to attempt to make a living from their skills because part of a man's pride came from supporting his family. For example, Sophia Jex-Blake's father grudgingly allowed her to teach maths, but not to accept a salary.[1] If her family fell upon hard times a middle class girl found few jobs open to her: generally, governess, schoolteacher or dressmaker. For working class women, whose skills were mainly domestic, there were plenty of jobs as servants and laundresses. Most of them lived in poverty despite working 10 to 16 hours a day. For example, although Joanna Taylor worked as a laundress in Hastings for 50 years she was unable to put anything aside for her old age and, when she became too old to work, she had to apply for parish relief.

The impressive list of occupations on pages 26 and 28 reflects the wide range of small businesses run by individual women and is not an accurate picture of the employment situation. In mid-Victorian Hastings, about 80% of working women were in just five occupations: domestic service, dressmaking, laundering, lodging house keeping and teaching.

There was no National Insurance, and no unemployment or other benefits. A woman either worked, was supported by someone, went on the streets or entered the workhouse. There were many friendly or benefit societies that offered a modicum of financial support to subscribers over short spells of illness or injury, but these were mainly for men. In the 1850s separate benefit clubs were established for each sex under the auspices of St Mary's parish. The St Mary's Female Assurance Society, which in 1858 was managed by Mrs. Hart, Campbell Cottage, East Hill, invited 'females whose time is money, and who, in sickness, can ill afford to lose that time' to join.

Occupations of women in Hastings & St Leonards 1830-1870
Part 2

nurse
nursemaid
outfitter
paper-flower maker
parlourmaid
pawnbroker
perfumier
pew opener
photographist
photographic artist
plumber/glazier/painter
printer
professor of singing
professor of music
professor of languages
pork butcher
poultry fancier
poulterer (licensed)
publican
pupil teacher
schoolmistress
school proprietor
secondhand clothes dealer
seamstress
sedan chair proprietor

sempstress
servants' registry office proprietor
shareholder
shell artiste/worker/dealer
shoebinder
shirtmaker
shrimp hawker
silk worker
silk weaver
slop seller
stationer
stay maker
straw hat maker
superintendent
tailoress
tallow chandler
tea dealer
tobacconist
toy dealer
undertaker
upholsterer
wardrobe dealer
washerwoman
watchmaker/mender
wine merchant

There is an enduring myth that all adult Victorian women were supported by their husbands but, in 1851, only 57% of women over 20 were married, 30% were unmarried and 13% were widows. Thus, 43% of women had no husband. Of these, roughly three-quarters of the spinsters, and one-quarter of the widows, were employed. In Hastings, of the 6675 women over 20, 54% were listed as 'dependent on relatives' and yet they often worked in their families' businesses. Of the remainder, just under 8% had private incomes and 38% (3059) were self-supporting.

Prior to the introduction of National Insurance in 1911, little documentary evidence existed in relation to employment and particularly to that of women. Most surviving records relate to areas of economic activity in which women rarely feature – for example income tax, apprenticeship indentures, pensions and civic appointments. Even the Census is not as useful or reliable as one might wish: it was taken only once every ten years, and employment that fell in between went unrecorded. The Censuses underestimate women's employment, partly because social factors led people to lie, and partly because enumerators omitted wives' work.[2]

According to Bessie Rayner Parkes, a contemporary specialist on female employment, the 1851 Census was incorrect about the percentage of married women in paid work, which it set at 22%. Parkes' own calculations found 37% to be a more accurate figure. She put the total number of women in paid employment in Britain at 3.1 million, or just over 44% of the female population.[3] Of these, 0.4 million were widows, 1.2 million were single and 1.5 million were married.[4]

While the Census should be treated with caution, it still provides the best available information regarding employment. The 1851 abstracts for Hastings reveal that there was no occupation, rank or calling in which the numbers of the sexes came even close to being equal. Men comprised 99% of labourers, 98% of the employees of national and local government and the learned professions, and 80% of those working with minerals or vegetables, and possessing or working the land. Women comprised three-quarters of those engaged in entertaining, making clothing, and performing personal offices, and two-thirds of those involved in literature, the fine arts and the sciences. Women were also 78% of the gentry, and 90% of the paupers.

WIVES & WIDOWS

The idea that 'married women did not work' is a fiction, so far as the poorer classes were concerned. Traditionally, all members of the family were involved in home-based trades, but the Industrial Revolution divided the sexes into 'breadwinner' and 'housewife'. Keeping his wife out of the workplace signified respectability for a man and gave him status. Although (as we shall see) this ideal was never achieved, it led people with pretensions to gentility to conceal wives' paid employment. The life of a working class

married woman depended on her husband's income. If he was a skilled worker she could devote herself to raising a family. If a trader, she might join him in business, childbearing permitting. But should she marry a labouring man, or one whose employment was seasonal or insecure or who was unable to work through infirmity or alcoholism, she might need to earn money throughout her married life.

The 1851 Census abstracts for Hastings record that, of 6,675 women over twenty, 43% were 'wives of no occupation'. The true figure was much lower, because Census enumerators were instructed that: 'The profession of wives ... living with their husband and assisting them ... need not be set down.' Because of this, the occupations of hundreds of wives working in family businesses are hidden from history. Only those employed in work distinctly unlike that of their husbands' were listed as occupied. To give but one example, Harriet Fisher of 56 High Street advertised and was listed in trade directories as a confectioner and other sources[5] confirm that she ran the shop; however, according to the Census, her husband was the confectioner and Harriet was 'unoccupied'.

Owing to the property laws and social customs, other official documents - such as deeds, directories, and licensing records – also fail to record the work of wives in family businesses, yet it was typical for them to work behind the scenes, stocktaking, ordering and bookkeeping. One was even her husband's chauffeuse. Anna Maria Savery married a busy Hastings surgeon in 1829, and 'was seen almost daily out driving with the doctor in his professional rounds, and taking command of the horse and carriage'.[6] It was customary for shops with male owners to be run by husband and wife. Records relating to licensed premises are particularly misleading in this respect. A pub or hotel was almost invariably run jointly by husband and wife and in some cases the wife had sole charge while the husband followed his own occupation. The same was true of some lodging-houses. In 1864 Mr. Brockwell, summonsed to court in relation to a lodging house registered in his name, explained that he knew nothing about the business, as it belonged to his wife while he worked elsewhere. Nevertheless, the law found him responsible.[7] Unusually, Priscilla Brown of 18 Shepherd Street is listed in the 1871 Census as a partner in her husband's business. He was a master-bricklayer employing three men.

It should not be supposed that married women worked only in dire financial circumstances. In Hastings many wives worked although their husbands appear to have been able to support them. Among dozens of examples were Elizabeth Woodgate, a lodging-house keeper whose husband was a master-builder employing five men, and egg-merchant Elizabeth Collins, who was married to a shoesmith. Most of them successfully combined careers with motherhood; indeed, Mrs. Collins had seven children. It is interesting to note that working mothers were so prevalent in mid-19th century Hastings that churches opened crèches specifically to cater for them.

MORTON'S

Wholesale and Retail China, Glass, and Staffordshire Warehouse,

43, HIGH STREET, AND CORNER OF COURTHOUSE STREET, HASTINGS.

H. M., in returning her sincere thanks to the Gentry, Inhabitants, and Visitors of Hastings, St. Leonards, and the vicinity, for the very liberal patronage she has received for the last sixteen years, respectfully begs to inform them she has recently made some VERY ADVANTAGEOUS PURCHASES in CHINA and GLASS, which will enable her to sell at Lower Prices than ever! The whole is of first-rate quality, and will be found, on inspection, at least 20 per cent. cheaper than any other house in the trade.

Without resorting to the usual practice of making long lists of Prices, H. M. would further observe that she has commenced selling at Wholesale Prices for Ready Money.

Several China Dessert sets, splendid patterns; ditto Burnished Gold ditto, very superb. The whole of these are well worth attention, as they are to be sold GREAT BARGAINS

Always on hand, a large assortment of Fancy Goods.

An early call is earnestly solicited.

☞ Please to observe the Address :—43, HIGH STREET, Close to the Town Clock.

The Victorian widow phenomenon

Perhaps the most powerful evidence of wives' involvement in their husbands' businesses is the universal practice of them taking over, automatically, after their husbands' death, even in industries considered 'unsuitable' for women, and in which women would not have been accepted in the open job market, either as employees or as apprentices. By widowhood, Hastings obtained a female butcher, a couple of licensed poulterers, a blacksmith, a cabinet maker, an undertaker, a plumber-glazier-painter and a fly proprietor. Widowhood explains how, in other towns, women are listed in Victorian trade directories as gas fitters and builders, although one assumes that they did not perform the labour themselves but supervised sons or employees. Caution, however, is urged in this respect.[8]

Charlotte Osborne, née Sargent, was involved in many retail enterprises in a 40-year career, as well as raising 13 children by two husbands. Directories first show her as a furniture seller at 43 George Street, and as a stationer at 27 Castle Street and Caroline Place. At 55 George Street she first opened a fruit shop and later a Berlin Wool and Fancy Repository in the 1850s. According to Brett, a Victorian chronicler of Hastings[9], her first husband was a cabinet maker, and her second a printer. She continued to run the printing business after his death in 1861, with her son as compositor. Charlotte died in 1898 at the age of 84.

Hannah Morton was one of the most successful female shopkeepers of mid-century Hastings. Born in 1806 in Derbyshire, she and her husband opened a china and glass business in Hastings. By 1841 she was a widow with children aged 2, 5 and 15. She moved from 27 High Street to larger premises at number 43 and opened new branches at 13 Castle Street and at 72 Norman Road, St Leonards, where her widowed daughter Mary Ann was manager. Mrs. Morton retired in 1877 and lived above 43 High Street until her death ten years later. Similarly, Harriet Ranger (b. 1802) married a master blacksmith and had five children. When he died, she took over and employed two smiths, one of whom was her son. This successful firm had branches in West Street, Shepherd Street and Longfield.[10]

Sarah Offen perhaps best exemplifies the hardworking, respectable, working class, mid-Victorian woman. She worked before and during her marriage, raised a family, and was widowed. She was born in Hertfordshire in 1810 and was servant to the Bird family at 31 Wellington Square, cook to Lady Lubbock, then cook-housekeeper to Lady Pilkington. She married in the late 1830s and leased 14 Undercliffe, letting it as apartments while raising her children. In 1841 the Offens opened a shop at 3 (now 35) Norman Road West, selling ironmongery, toys and earthenware. Just three years later, Sarah was widowed, and she ran the shop alone for 15 years. This 'cheerful and chatty old townswoman' died in 1887.[11]

Left one of Hannah Morton's advertisements in a trade directory and a receipt from her shop, dated 1861. *Receipt reproduced by courtesy of Hastings Museums and Art Gallery.*

BED & BOARD

Offering accommodation in their own homes is an ancient and traditional occupation of women. During the late 18th century Hastings gained favour among the fashionable and wealthy as a watering-place, and the small handful of hotels was soon unable to cope with the growing number of visitors. Women with a spare room or two – especially on the seafront – saw an opportunity to make money, and the seaside landlady was born. Offering accommodation was an ideal business for women: it was socially-acceptable, it utilised their existing domestic skills and, as an added return, it taught them business skills and book-keeping.

As Hastings' popularity grew women were not slow in recognising the enormous business opportunities in this area. Some opened lodging- and boarding-houses; others took employment as lodging-house keepers. By 1817 Powell's Guide listed over 80 women offering all types of accommodation, from a homely single bedroom to a seven-room beach house. Some let rooms in addition to following a trade or business of their own: milliner Mrs. Henbury let seven bedrooms in her High Street home; while for others it was their only source of income: Miss Dutton ran a ten-bedroom boarding-house with three reception rooms. In the Priory Valley, Miss Browning rather cannily opened a boarding-house near the new *Castle Hotel*, while Mrs. Boomer and Mrs. Gallop offered rooms near the Rope Walk on the America Ground. In 1832, Eliza Savage was one of the first women to open a boarding house in Wellington Square, at no. 43.

The establishment of St Leonards in 1828 brought women further opportunities and as early as 1830, several were offering seafront accommodation; one was Ann Thorp, at 20 Grand Parade.[12] Mrs. Thompson's at Marina offered 'all the comforts of a private residence with the additional advantage of select society and an excellent table'.[13] Miss Woodgate came to St Leonards in 1829 as a lady's maid. After the death of her employer, she leased 19 and 20 Marina and ran them as lodging houses for 45 years.

A boarding house was like a hotel, with bedrooms and communal reception rooms whereas in lodging-houses serviced apartments were let. Some house-owners employed women (and sometimes men) to manage the premises, on a commission-basis or for a weekly wage. Others leased and managed a house themselves. By 1851, running a lodging- or boarding-house was the most populous occupational category of businesswomen in Hastings. There were 126 women listed and many more unlisted. Women attained a near-monopoly on the seafront: numbers 1, 2, 4, 5, 7, 8, 9, 10 and 11 Battery and at 1, 2, 3, 4, 6, 8, 11 and 12 Parade were all lodging-houses run by women.

The job required organisational as well as domestic skills; it involved shopping, laundry, cooking and cleaning and also heavy lifting - buckets of coal and jugs of hot water had to be carried up many stairs, and seafront houses were up to six storeys high. In every bedroom, fire-grates had to be cleaned and dirty water removed. Keepers of the larger houses employed servant girls to perform these tasks.

COMFORTABLE LODGINGS

'This is Your Bed, Sir.'

Punch magazine's depiction of a female lodging house keeper in the 1860s.

A RESPECTABLE MARRIED WOMAN, WITHOUT ENCUMBRANCE, wishes for the care of a Lodging-House, in Hastings or St. Leonards, or elsewhere. She is a good Cook, and can give good references. Address, J. R., 1, Sussex place, St. Leonards-on-Sea.

Lodging-house keepers were the mainstay of the tourist and visitor trade and their excellence contributed greatly to the commercial success of the town. Those in Hastings were so highly respected that in 1884 R. E. Smith MP argued that they deserved the vote. He must have been referring to the top end of the market because the title 'lodging-house' included every class of establishment from the sublime to the squalid. The former included the 13 elegant seaside residences known as Pelham Crescent. Twelve were lodging houses, of which nine were run by women. Elizabeth Ellis, landlady at no. 10 in the 1860s, engaged her three daughters to help manage the house. These sumptuously-furnished houses were let by the year, season or month to professional men such as doctors, clergymen, JPs and MPs.

While in 1820 demand for lodgings had outstripped supply, by the 1860s the reverse was true. Landladies had to lower their charges, and some of them even went out of business. Angela Hanson of 88 Marina went bankrupt in 1863, owing £320 to 33 businesses. Most were local tradesmen with whom she had accumulated large accounts, in accordance with the custom of the day: she owed £45 to her grocer – about 45 times the average weekly wage. However, the only debt the court ordered her to settle was the £7. 10s she owed to her manservant. She did not own the house, and selling all her furniture raised only £57. [14] Angela's debts were small compared with those of Ann Ward, who owed over £2,000 when her lodging-house at Robertson Terrace failed in 1866. Yet, for some, business was thriving: Elizabeth Cox simultaneously kept five lodging houses at Eversfield Place and Robertson Terrace.

At the other end of the scale, tramp lodging-houses catered for the near-destitute, hawkers and travellers. As fuller descriptions of these premises and their inmates will be included in *Down & Out in Victorian Hastings* (forthcoming), they are dealt with only briefly here. All were located in the Old Town, and most were tucked away behind public houses or in narrow passages known as twittens. Landladies either rented the house, paid the expenses and kept the income; or they managed the house on behalf of the owner, with whom they shared the income 50/50. Many landladies performed all the cooking and washing for their lodgers. There were several premises in East Hill Passage, including Ellen Lester's, which was above her beer-shop, *The Fisherman's Home*[15] and Esther Brooker's, which accommodated 26 guests on Census night 1851, most of whom were travellers. Sarah Fuller's, 12 Wellington Court, was a squalid place just behind the *King's Head*. Another two were located behind the *Crown Inn*. One of these, the *Merry Christmas*,[16] was managed at one time by Catherine Adams and later by Eliza Paris, who employed a man to help her deal with rough customers. She rented the premises for 7s a week, plus taxes, and let 24 beds at 2s a week each. Another, with 12 beds, was run by Mrs. Huggett, who paid the landlord half of the income. She charged 2s per week from which she 'found' (paid for) all the coals and candles.[17] Fisher's had 16 beds and the Principal, Mrs. Emily Brockwell, paid 7s 6d a week rent for it. She later took premises in Gibbon Square, behind the *King's Head*. Ann Holt rented a tramp lodging house behind the *Cinque Port Arms* in All Saint's St.

THE SWAN HOTEL was, on Friday, visited by a school party of about fifty, who came from Merton, Surrey, in charge of the Rev. Henry Balchin. The party visited the Castle ruins and other places of interest, and returned to the Swan for dinner and tea. So well satisfied were the managers with Mrs. Carswell's arrangements, that they promised to pay her another visit next year, in lieu of going to Brighton.—To-morrow the printers from the establishment of Messrs. Waterlow and Son, the railway and parliamentary typographers, take up their quarters at the Swan, for a two or three days' visit.

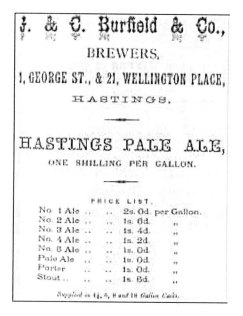

Following the deaths of brothers James and Charles Burfield, their brewery and associated retail businesses came into the hands of their widows Kate and Frances, who ran them for many years without changing the name of the company from *J & C Burfield*. This obscured the fact that this advertisement was for a business owned and run by women. The 1871 Census entry for 1, George Street shows Kate Burfield, a widow of 62 as *Head of Household*, her occupation as *Brewer employing 15 men*. A daughter and son are listed as *brewers manager* while another son was an *assistant*.

She charged the inmates 2s a week for bed, washing and cooking, and hired a keeper to perform all the work. There were two dormitories, each accommodating eight persons. When full the income was 32s a week, from which Miss Holt paid 12s rent and paid the keeper's wage of about 10s.

Miss Holt was a respectable businesswoman with a thriving stationer's shop on the seafront, but often the owners were more disreputable than the inmates. Mary Griffin of Waterloo Place was charged with begging in 1860 and was sent to Lewes Gaol for seven days; a year later she was charged with being drunk and disorderly and fined 5s. Mrs. Fisher was fined for overcrowding her lodging-house in East Bourne Street and the servant, Sarah Hart, was fined 5s for being drunk and incapable.

One interesting character was Bridget Flannagan (b. 1816), who married a railway navvy. Both were Irish, and their migration can be tracked from the birthplaces of their three children: Bristol, Tunbridge Wells, and Ore. Bridget was an enterprising woman who saw a profitable opportunity in the slums of the Old Town when her husband's job brought them to Hastings in 1850: he was employed in building the railway extension from St Leonards to Hastings. Bridget was no respecter of the law: after being fined for running an unlicensed common lodging house at the Fishmarket, called the *Baker's Arms*, she opened a legitimate one in Waterloo Passage but was later fined £1 for failing to whitewash the house, 1s for allowing more persons to sleep in one room than the law permitted, and 1s for permitting persons of opposite sexes to sleep in the same room.

LANDLADIES & LICENSEES

The provision of accommodation and alcohol were intermingled: most pubs and beer-shops offered rooms, and hotels were licensed to sell alcohol. Women have been involved in these trades for centuries and it is, therefore, impossible to trace the first female innkeeper in Hastings.

Licensing began in 1610 and, from the start, some were issued to single women and widows. Records from the 1820s show that to obtain a license, a person had to enter into recognizances with sureties of £30 from themselves and £10 each from two persons of good social standing, generally other trades-people. In 1828, of the 17 licensed premised in Hastings, three were licensed to women. By 1841 over 10,000 British women held liquor licenses for breweries, victuallers, refreshment rooms, hotels, public houses and beer-shops. Licenses were issued by magistrates and renewed yearly. The Bench received petitions of objection or support from locals. For example, Ann Tolhurst of Ore was refused a beer-shop license after complaints that her apple-shop was an unsuitable premises for the beer trade.

In 1862 Hastings & St Leonards contained 62 public houses and 44 beer shops. About half of all beer-shops and about one in 10 public houses were licensed to women. However, when a married man was granted a license, his wife became the pub landlady and was treated as such.

Some public houses licensed to women of Victorian Hastings. *Clockwise from top left: The Hastings Arms*, 2 George Street, whose licensees included Ann Thwaites, Ann Sargent and Mary Ann Ray. The *Albion Hotel,* licensed to Harriet Bowles, Mrs. Ellis and Susan Emary. The former *Duke of York*, Union Street, St Leonards, licensed to Mary Fairhall. The former *George Inn*, 120 All Saints' Street, licensed in the 1830s to Rebecca Furby and in the 1850s to Rebecca Wood. *The Stag*, All Saints' Street, licensed to Philly Jenkins and owned by Mary Heathfield.

Only one example was discovered of a couple holding a joint license: Mr. & Mrs. Wenham of the *Duke of Cornwall,* Post Office Passage. Although law and custom dictated that the husband must be the licensee, to all intents and purposes, these were joint businesses. There is plenty of evidence to support this. If accommodation was let, it was the wife who managed the rooms, meals and laundry. When external catering was undertaken, more often than not the customer praised the wife for the excellence of the victuals. When a publican was charged with breaching licensing laws, it was often his wife who appeared in court, and paid the fine.

Sometimes the wife took charge during the licensee's absence. Jane Cox ran the *Dun Horse* beer-shop single-handedly from 1857 to 1860, yet her invalid husband held the license. Only on his death was the license transferred to her. It was also common for a wife to take sole charge of the business while the licensee followed his own career; for example, Mr. Nabbs was a sailmaker while his wife Sarah ran the *Pilot Inn.*[18]

Wife-landladies are very difficult to trace because their names are absent from records, directories and advertisements. This rest of this section therefore focuses on single women and widows who were licensees and proprietresses in their own right.

Hoteliers

One of the earliest hotels, *The Crown,* Courthouse Street, was run by widow Sarah Smith between 1815 and 1832. It was a coaching inn, with stabling all the way up Crown Lane to Tackleway. Powell's Guide of 1831 remarked that 'Mrs. Smith deserves particular commendation and support, as being the first (with a family of seven children) to add to the accommodation of Visitors by every species of comfort, neatness, and domestic attention'. The *Conqueror Hotel,*[19] one of the earliest in St Leonards, was managed by Mrs. Collins in the 1830s before the license was transferred to Mrs. Sarah Johnson, who was held in high regard: Robert Hollond MP chose to stay there on many occasions, and she was contracted to provide the catering for a huge political banquet in 1841, held in a series of marquees on Priory Meadows. Brett recalled that

> after carrying on the hotel for some time with remarkable energy, [she] converted it into a boarding house. Even then, the success of the establishment was perhaps less thorough than its spirited proprietress desired, and, as this was not the only estate in St Leonards over which she had command, the original *Conqueror* became a *Brunswick* in other hands and was further reduced to the rank of a private lodging house, and later run by Mrs. Gates'.[20]

The four most prestigious hotels of 19th century Hastings - the *Royal Oak,* the *Swan,* the *Castle* and the *Albion* - all had female proprietors at some point.

The Bull at Bulverhythe, an old coaching inn, was licensed in 1827 to Hannah Davis, in 1833 to Elizabeth Wilkinson and in the 1840s to Miss Sheather.

The Castle Hotel in the 1820s. Around 1854-55 Miss Frances Emary was the proprietress and licensee.

The first *Royal Oak* was at Oak Hill, at the southern end of the High Street.[21] After this closed a second *Royal Oak* was opened at Castle Street,[22] with Ann Sargent as licensee from 1825 until 1829; she had been licensee of the *Hastings Arms* from 1821-2. In 1835, Mr. & Mrs. Yates took over, having previously run the *Hare & Hounds* at Ore.[23] Ann Yates (née Pearson) was a hotel and pub landlady from 1832 until 1864 during which time she gave birth to 13 children, of whom six died in infancy. Two daughters worked in the hotel as barmaids. Although three out of the four family members running the pub were female, as William Yates was licensee only his name is recorded and documented. After his death in 1864, Ann took over the license but by the end of the year she had retired. She moved to London, but retained ownership of the *Royal Oak,* which she leased to subsequent licensees, one of whom was Alice Darke, who appears in the 1871 Census as its licensee at the surprisingly young age of 22.

The *Swan Hotel* had for centuries been Hastings' foremost coaching inn, public house and hotel, enjoying a prominent position in the High Street. Every important social and civic function was held there, including sumptuous dinners, fascinating lectures and glittering musical entertainments. Among its licensees were at least six women, including Mrs. Hay (1642), Mercy Grove (1726-29), Widow Gurr (1751) and Henrietta Collier (c. 1836-1841).

The hey-day of the *Swan* was the mid-19th century. Its finest hour came when it was chosen as the venue for a famous banquet in 1850 in honour of the Lord Mayor of London, a native of Hastings. Incidentally, according to written accounts, no women were present, and a sketch[24] in the *Illustrated London News* confirms this. Secondary sources habitually cite William Carswell's name in connection with the *Swan* in the 19th century, yet his wife Elizabeth was landlady for over 30 years while her husband was landlord for 17 years. After his death in 1858 his estate passed to his wife, who was granted a transfer of license. Under her management, the *Swan* maintained its high reputation and in 1859 it was chosen to provide a magnificent banquet in honour of the Bishop of Chichester and 80 other dignitaries.

The *Swan Tap,* a beer-shop with accommodation which adjoined the *Swan,* was run in the 1860s by Miss Mary Rosina Willett. It was known to attract undesirables, and the landlady was criticised by magistrates for allowing four people, two of each sex, to share a room for a fortnight. Although Mrs. Carswell had no control over the *Tap,* it operated under the license she held for the *Swan,* rendering her legally responsible for its conduct, a situation criticised by some as unfair to the licensee.

In 1871 Elizabeth Carswell received a special presentation from prominent townspeople on the occasion of her 30th anniversary as landlady. In November 1872, she applied to magistrates for a permit to remain open till midnight for the forthcoming Mayor's Banquet. The Mayor himself heard the application - and declined it![25] Owing to ill-health Mrs. Carswell retired in 1873 and died a year later at her home, 9 High Street, leaving her estate to her sister and nieces. The vacant tenancy, advertised in the local

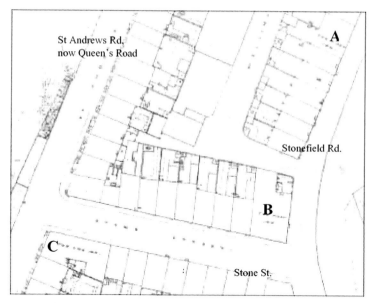

St Andrews Rd, now Queen's Road

A

Stonefield Rd.

B

C

Stone St.

Above 1850s map showing (A) the *Tiger*, (B) the *Pilot* and (C) the *Lion* inns, all of which had female licensees in the mid-19th century. All three still stand. The *Tiger* closed in 1930 and, like the *Pilot*, is now a private house. The *Lion* is now a shop and a dwelling. *Below* Mary Glyde lost her fly (taxi-cab) business when she went bankrupt, but she retained her beer-shop.

THE BANKRUPTCY ACT, 1861.

In the County Court of Sussex holden at Hastings·

IN the matter of MARY GLYDE, of No. 4, Hill-street, Hastings, in the County of Sussex, Fly Proprietress and Beerhouse-keeper, adjudged Bankrupt on the 26th day of July, 1866.

A Meeting of the Creditors of the said Bankrupt will be held before the Registrar at the County Court Office, Hastings, on the 18th day of December, 1866, at Eleven o'clock in the forenoon, for the purpose of declaring a dividend, and also whether any allowance shall be made to the bankrupt. Proofs of debts will be received, and Creditors who have not yet proved, and do not then prove, will be excluded the benefit of the dividend.

WILLIAM BLACKMAN YOUNG,
Registrar.

newspaper, was taken by Mrs. Collins, a lady with a great liking for strong liquor. In 1875, she was summonsed for assaulting her husband.[26]

The first serious rival to the *Swan* opened in 1817 as *Emary's Castle Inn Family Hotel.* Situated on the corner of Wellington Place, facing the foot of the West Hill, it was the first major hotel to open in Hastings 'new town'.[27] It had Assembly Rooms for fashionable gatherings and public meetings, a prototype tourist information facility, coach-houses, stables, and a well. Coaches for London and Brighton left from its doorstep. The name of James Emary is always mentioned in connection with the *Castle*, but from 1854-55 his daughter Frances was proprietor,[28] at which time it was called *The Castle Hotel & Posting House.* In 1871, Maria E. Lock, a widow aged 47, was the hotel's manager and on Census night she had eight guests and 13 live-in staff in her charge.

Hastings' fourth important hotel, the *Albion*, was in the ownership of the Emarys until James Emary ceased all connection with it (and with the *Castle*) in 1867. The license went first to Harriet Bowles, then to Mr. Ellis, whose constant inebriation rendered him unable to conduct the house and Harriet Bowles was engaged as manager. In 1869 the license was transferred to his mother, as he was no longer a suitable person. By the 1880s the *Albion* was back in the hands of the Emarys, with James' widow Susan as licensee.

Other hotels with female proprietors included:

Priory Family Hotel, 24 Robertson Street, Misses Mary & Ellen Eldridge (1850s)
Railway & Commercial Hotel, 20 Havelock Road, Miss Mary Eldridge (1850s)
Commercial Hotel and Dining Rooms, 20 Havelock Road, Mrs. Mary Ann Linney (1871)
Provincial Hotel, 18 Havelock Road, Mary Ann Montague (1871)
Belle Vue Hotel, 47 East Parade, Louisa Longhurst (1871)
Duke of York, 5 Union Road, St Leonards, Mrs. Mary Fairhall (1871)
Green's Family Hotel, 1 Havelock Road, Eliza Green (1860s & 1870s)

The *Duke of York* was a low-class hotel in a crowded working class area. Mary Fairhall's sister, daughter and two sons also worked on the premises. The only guests when the 1871 Census was taken were 10 musicians – presumably, a visiting band.[29]

Beer-shops & Public-houses

Ale-brewing and vending is an ancient female trade. Until the late 19th century, there were few 'soft' drinks available and water was mainly unfit to drink, so it was customary for beer to be taken freely at any time of the day, and by both sexes, at least amongst the labouring classes. A limited license, which excluded spirits, was given by justices. Mary Makings was

A DISORDERLY BEER-HOUSE.—*Harriet Vinall*, a widow, was summoned on the complaint of Superintendent Glenister, for knowingly permitting drunkenness and disorderly conduct in her licensed house, on Sunday, the 25th Feb.—Superintendent Glenister said the defendant kept the Britannia beer-house, in Bourne-street.—Defendant said the parties did not get drunk in her house.—The Clerk said that was not the charge. She was summoned for allowing drunkenness in her house.—Defendant said she was not guilty.—Superintendent Glenister said he should prove that nearly all the whole of Sunday there was one continual noise, disturbance, fighting, and drunkenness in the house. At a quarter to four the police were called in by the neighbours, and in the back kitchen they found six men and three or four women. Two were drunk, and the rest were the worse for liquor. One of the men had his clothes off, and was bleeding from the face; one of the women had a black eye, 5 panes of glass were broken, and it was one scene of disorder.—Police-Constable Dennis proved these facts, and Charles Moore, who lives next door, and another neighbour, gave evidence of the disorder which prevailed. Very foul language was used.—Defendant said she tried all she could to stop it. The noise broke out in a moment, but it lasted only a few minutes, and was not continued from half-past two till five o'clock, as was alleged.—Elizabeth Williams was called for defendant, and said the parties were all lodgers. There was a dispute, and defendant tried to quell it. No beer was drawn.—George Brannagan was called, but did not assist the case for the defendant.—Superintendent Glenister said there had previously been cautions given. It was a tramps' lodging-house, and he had not, therefore, the same supervision over it as he had over other houses. Beer could be supplied to the tramps at any time, Sundays included. Other houses would be proceeded against, if no improvement took place. He did not wish to press this case harshly.—Defendant was fined 40s., and costs 18s., or a month's imprisonment.—Allowed till next day for payment.—Mr. Putland said such houses were a disgrace to the town.

1866 press cutting telling a typical tale of a disorderly beer-shop.

refused one in 1796 and three years later was convicted of selling ale and beer unlicensed.[30] An Act of Parliament in 1830 provided that any householder assessed to the poor rate could obtain a license from the Excise for a fee of two guineas, which allowed the sale of beer from private houses, for consumption on or off the premises. From 1869, a justices' licence was again required.

The first woman beer-seller in St Leonards was Mrs. Towner, who in 1829 sold small-beer - for which no license was required - to the workmen of architect and town founder James Burton. By the mid-19th century, about half of all Hastings beer-shop licenses were held by women. Most were low-class places, often located in residential areas. Beer-shops near the seafront opened as early as 3.30am to cater for fishermen. Some offered music and dancing, and much drunken quarrelling was conducted inside and out - much to the annoyance of neighbours, and many were frequented by prostitutes, who often lodged in rooms above. A local newspaper editor described beer-shops as 'a greater source of public evil than the public-houses' and suggested their abolition.[31]

In 1867, beer-shop keeper Jane Cox applied for an upgrade in her license to public-house status. She had run the *Dun Horse* for ten years. For the first three years her husband was the licensee but, as he was mentally ill, she had run the business alone and, when he died, the license had been transferred to her. She was supporting four small children and wanted to widen her scope to sell spirits. The license was granted and it became a pub.

Public houses

Women were licensees of all types of premises, from large, prominent and respectable houses in fashionable shopping streets, to run-down and rowdy 'gin palaces' crowded with low-class customers. Among the former were the *Hastings Arms* in George Street, which had at least three female licensees in the 19th century: Ann Thwaites, 1800-04; Ann Sargent 1821-24 and Mary Ann Ray 1870-71. Mrs. Thwaites later went on to open the *Anchor* at 13 George St, while Mrs. Sargent later took the *Royal Oak*. *The Angel*, St Mary's Terrace, was licensed to Miss Barbara Ticehurst in 1852. It was regularly patronised by the artist Whistler, who painted the now world-famous portrait of his mother in her house at no. 43. The pub was built above St Clement's Caves, which were used at some point as its cellars. *The Bull*, an old coaching inn, was licensed in 1827 to Hannah Davis, widow of the previous landlord. Miss Sheather was licensee in the 1840s, during an exceptionally busy and profitable period in the history of the pub: the newly-opened railway line from Eastbourne terminated nearby, and passengers had to wait for a coach and horses to take them on to Hastings.

MILLINERY AND DRESSMAKING.

MRS. LYE

Returns her sincere thanks for the very liberal support she has received in the above part of her business, and hopes, by punctuality and moderate charges to merit a continuance of their support.

Mrs. L. begs to submit the following low scale of charges:—

	s.	d.
Making Plain Dress - - - - -	3	0
" Flounced ditto - - - - -	4	6
" Mantles - - - - - -	1	9
" Drawn Bonnets - - - - -	3	0

Drawn Silk Bonnets, from 4s. 6d. to 7s. 6d.
Black Silk Mantles, from 10s. 6d.

—o—

The Show Room is now replete with every novelty for the season.

Mourning and Wedding Orders attended to with the greatest despatch.

ADDRESS.---14, ROBERTSON STREET.

N.B.,---Mrs. DAY, from 36, High Street, removed to the above Establishment.

At all levels of the liquor trade, proprietors frequently were summonsed to court for infringements of their licenses. In the majority of cases, it was simply a case of being open out of hours. Even respectable hotelier Eliza Green of *Green's Family Hotel*, opposite Hastings station, was fined a shilling in 1860 for selling alcohol at 11:30am on a Sunday, during the hours of Divine service. Policemen in plain clothes would sometimes keep watch on premises they suspected. One Sunday morning in 1874, three officers were watching Philly Jenkins' *Tiger Inn* in Stonefield Street. Two visited her briefly and, when they left, a plain-clothes man on watch saw a woman enter at 10:55am. He followed her and saw a quart of beer in an earthenware jug, and 6d on the counter. Jenkins was summonsed for selling beer 5 minutes early. The women concocted an unconvincing tale: Mary Ann Snashall, of 15 Stonefield Street, who had worked casually for Jenkins for 14 years, had come in to assist with changing the beer barrels. The beer in the jug was dregs from the dwindling barrel. The 6d on the counter had been left by a boy to whom she earlier gave change. Jenkins was fined £1 and Snashall, 10s.[32] Licensees were more frequently fined for being open late. Elizabeth Cull, of the *Old House at Home Beer-house*, 44 All Saints Street, was given a token fine in 1872 for being open after 11pm, but when she was unable to produce her license she was fined a hefty £10.

An offence which could lose a landlady her license was 'suffering divers persons of notoriously bad character to assemble'. Such a charge was brought against Mrs. Harriet Perigoe of the *White Lion*, 7 St Michael's Terrace, in 1872. A policeman spotted two prostitutes – Miss Carey and Miss Thompsett - entering private rooms with men. When magistrates heard that the house was 'notorious' and of a 'most disorderly character', and that this summons was not the first, Perigoe was fined £2. 10s plus 15s costs, which she paid at once. Mary Ann Ray, who was granted the transfer of the license of the *Hastings Arms* on her husband's death in 1870, was summonsed on a similar charge. The pub had been well-conducted under Mr. Ray but the police had warned Mary about the type of clientele beginning to congregate there. Soon, the place was full of prostitutes and one had robbed a man. Mary said such characters entered the pub when she was out, or slipped in by the back door while the pub was busy, and she and her daughters could not see them from behind the bar. The police considered her 'unable to conduct a house of this description' and the magistrate fined her £1. Within a year she had ceased to run the pub.

Some women licensees were also freeholders of the pub or beer-house; others were freeholders who let the premises to a licensee; a document in Hastings Museum lists 20 women deriving income in this way.

Victuallers

A few women in mid-century Hastings ran non-licensed catering establishments. Mary Church owned a coffee house at 2 London Road, St Leonards while Ann Hyland had an eating house at 29 George Street.

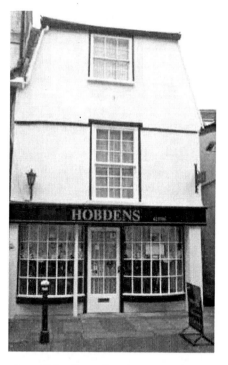

Above 33 West Street, from where Sophia Abbot ran a successful business as a tea dealer, "the most genteel of provision trades". The building is now Grade II listed.

Ann Hyland's eating house used to occupy this building, 29 George Street – now a listed building.

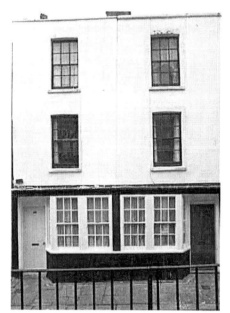

Left Another listed building, 102-103 All Saint's Street. Its Victorian occupiers included Mary White, grocer, and Eliza Paris, greengrocer. *Below* Typical mid-century shop front attracting customers wearing the typical dresses of the era.

One of Hastings' foremost licensed victuallers was Miss Ann Lock. She expanded her high-class confectionery shop at 50½ George Street into a refreshment room and obtained a license so she could offer brandy. Miss Lock's was 'frequented by a higher class, and at higher prices' than other cafés.[33] In 1864 she was commissioned to make a wedding cake for Catherine, daughter of Hastings' MP Frederick North. The following year she provided the refreshments for the town's Grand Christmas Society Ball in the Assembly Rooms at St Leonards, and in 1866 she was engaged to provide a sumptuous wedding breakfast for the marriage of Mr. North's niece. The 1871 Census showed that she employed three men and that her mother, the widow of a tailor, lived with her.

Brewers

Three women owned commercial breweries in mid-century Hastings. In the 1850s Mrs. Ellen Ruth Amoore (née Fermor) took over the Eagle Brewery after her husband's death. The Phoenix Brewery in Courthouse Street, owned by the Burfield brothers, passed in the late 1860s to their widows, Kate and Frances. In 1872 they also owned 11 public houses and 3 beer-shops.[34] The rental from these, together with the brewery, must have brought a considerable income. According to the 1871 Census, Kate employed 15 men in the Phoenix Brewery, where her two sons and daughter Harriet were managers. They lived at 1, George Street.

SHOPS & SERVICES

Records dating back to the beginning of the 19th century show many female retailers and dealers operating in Hastings. They were particularly involved in selling food and clothing. For instance, several women ran millinery and dressmakers' shops and, in 1826, women held five of the 24 stalls at the Town Fair. Three out of the four fishmongers in town in 1826 were female; more unusually, Miss Abbott of West Street was a tea dealer – 'the most "genteel" of all the provision trades'.[35]

During the period 1830-1870 a wide range of goods was sold by women, including coal, tobacco, eggs, milk, toys, second hand clothing, baby linen, earthenware, furniture, shells, wool, fancy goods, poultry, fish, fruit, lace, hats, china, stationery and books. Women were cowkeepers, confectioners, butchers, bakers, grocers, pawnbrokers, seed dealers and ironmongers. In 1864, two widows – Mrs. Stace and Mrs. Polhill, held licenses to sell game. Mrs. Pears was quite a jill-of-all-trades: she was a milliner and dressmaker, and proprietress of a fancy toy shop, a stay and crinoline warehouse and a registry office for servants. Four female tea dealers were trading in Hastings between 1830 and 1860.

By 1861, women were the majority of shopkeepers in Hastings. Almost 40% of shops were listed in the name of a sole proprietress. The rest were listed in men's names, but most were family businesses. English property law prevented a married woman from owning a business and social custom, coupled with what Helen Taylor [36] called women's 'timidity

and dread of exposing their names to public observation', dictated that only the husband's name be used for publicity, for example advertisements, guides and directories, although a few disregarded this. Evidence from dozens of court cases in which male proprietors sued shoplifters verifies that wives managed the shop.

Middle-class women with capital opened high-class shops in fashionable areas, usually selling millinery, mainly to lady clients. Working-class women's speciality was provision shops, a great many of which were in the Old Town, where many buildings were run-down, and tiny cottages were crowded along narrow roads. These small shops depended heavily on the fishing industry, and a poor catch or a tragedy at sea had a huge knock-on effect upon them.

While some female shopkeepers engaged men - for example, Mrs. Winifred Stubberfield (b.1810) employed three male assistants[37] in her grocery shop at 11 London Road - most shop assistants were young females, often the daughters, granddaughters or nieces of the proprietress. Even Thomas Brett, whose chronicles are cited often in this book, employed his daughter Augusta in his bookshop at 28 Norman Road West.

Women ran businesses both as sole traders and in partnerships. In the 1860s, four sisters - Millicent, Maria, Marian and Matilda - managed (and lived above) a corset and stay shop at 16 Wellington Place, which was owned by their father, Mr. Greenaway. Widows Sarah Daniel and Mary Jeffrey, stay-makers, were partners, as were shopkeeper sisters Eliza and Jane Smith. Stationer Ann Holt was in business with her younger brother from 1838 until the 1870s and straw bonnet manufacturers Louisa and Jane Pollard were mother and daughter. Harriet Waters, a spinster, and Elizabeth Northery, a widow, ran a successful ladies' outfitters in Robertson Street in the 1860s, when it was known as 'the Regent Street of Hastings'. The pair resided above the shop with Elizabeth's two children, a girl shop assistant and a house-servant. One business was passed from mother to daughter to grand-daughter over a period of 70 years: around 1824 Mrs. Oliver opened a fancy shell shop at 6 East Beach Street. She was 'a woman of great size' who 'was regarded as a celebrity by the visitors' and whose first customer was reputed to have been Lady Byron, divorced wife of the poet. Mrs. Oliver died in 1854 whereupon her daughter, Mrs. Dine, carried on the business. When she died in 1888, she passed on the business to her unmarried daughter.[38] Ann Golding ran a fruiterer's shop at 16 George Street, from where she sold the produce of her husband's market-garden. Ann, known as 'Nanny', died in 1873 leaving the business to her two daughters, who relocated it to 31 White Rock Place.

Commercial Services

Women were employed by commercial firms and private individuals as caretakers in establishments open to the public. There were many female gate-keepers and toll-collectors in Britain. Among the Hastings gate-keepers were Mary Beany at Baldslow House, a widow with three young

children, and elderly spinster Elizabeth Whybourne at Bohemia Lodge, who still held the job in 1871 at the age of 96. Brett mentions that, in the early 19th century, 'There presided in the Tower toll-gate[39] a venerable old dame and doctress of the name of Dabney ... much respected by all who knew her'.[40] Tollgate Collectors in the 1860s and 70s included Sarah Dawe of 84 St Andrew's Road,[41] Julia Missen of St Leonards Green, Eliza Pelling of Tower House and Eliza Graves of 4 Albert Crescent, South Road.

The Earl of Chichester employed a woman as Keeper of Old Hastings Castle in the 1850s. Widow Sarah Whyborne, a lady in her sixties, was assisted by her son, who later succeeded her. She kept a resident house-servant, so presumably the Earl paid a reasonable wage. During the 1850s, fruiterer Ann Golding, mentioned above, was also listed in directories and advertisements as 'Keeper of St Clement's Caves and Cosmorama'. Her husband had rediscovered the caves in 1825 and obtained permission to open them as a tourist attraction in 1827. When Ann died, her daughters took over the caves. In the 1870s, Charlotte Moore was proprietor of both the Central Arcade in Havelock Road and of the Pelham Arcade, both very busy and fashionable shopping areas.

Several women were bathing machine proprietors. One of them, Ann Cobby, was one of the great 'characters' of Hastings beach. Records of her presence, at her 'patch' opposite Breed's Place, span 17 years around the middle of the century. In 1854 she was paid £5 by Hastings Commissioners for her expenses in 'breaking the rocks off the Parade to get the machine out' after town improvements blocked her exit. She and her family were a rough lot, by all accounts, regularly involved in arguments and brawls, usually with each other, which frequently landed them in the magistrates' court.[42] Following a complaint by a gentleman, Mrs. Cobby was summonsed in 1865 for 'cruelly torturing her horse by causing it to be worked in an unfit state'. She vehemently denied the charge, asserting that she had owned horses for many years and always looked after them well. Fined 2s 6d and 13s costs, Mrs. Cobby left the court enraged: 'It won't stop there; 'I don't see why my character should be taken away by a gentleman like him'.[43] Resentments simmered between rival bathing machines, and sporadic outbreaks of violence were reported in the local press.

Several women were proprietors and managers of commercial indoor baths. The earliest was possibly Mrs Neal, manager of the Old Baths in about 1830. Those at Pelham Place opened in 1825 with 'excellent plunging and shampooing.' They were located just east of the Crescent, and were intended for the well-to-do visitor. A stone hall led into 'two handsome saloons, of an octagonal form and decorated with beautiful Chinese scenery'.[44] The proprietor at mid-century was Mrs. Martha Thatcher, succeeded on her death in 1857 by her daughter Ellen. By the 1870s, Pelham Baths were in the hands of Mrs. Jane Emary and her daughters, whose family had owned the *Castle* and *Albion* hotels. The baths in the basement of the Assembly Rooms (now the Masonic Hall) were run by Mr. & Mrs. Barnes. The Royal Baths, opposite the *Royal Victoria Hotel*, were managed by Philadelphia Roberts and her husband in the 1830s[45] then by Mr. & Mrs. Cozens and, in the 1870s, by widow Mrs. Margaret Parker.

Women were also employed in bathing establishments as bathers, and in the Turkish Baths as shampooers, to attend only to lady clients.

The aforementioned Martha and Ellen Thatcher were also consecutive proprietresses of a Theological Society and Library located on the baths premises.[46] But they were not the first Hastings women to run a library; in 1817, Mrs. Austin opened one within the Marine Library and also offered accommodation there.

Therapeutic hypnotherapy may sound like a modern-day 'alternative' treatment but it existed in the 19th century, under the name 'curative mesmerism'. A lady practitioner resided in Hastings in the 1860s, having been trained at the Mesmeric Infirmary in London. She advertised anonymously in the local press, and could be contacted 'c/o Homeopathic Chemist, Robertson Street.' Women were not permitted to train in the medical profession; however, a great many unqualified nurses and midwives operated in Hastings, relying on experience and traditional remedies handed down from mothers and grandmothers. In 1879, the world's first qualified female doctor, Elizabeth Blackwell, retired to Hastings.[47]

A few women worked in transport. In 1836, Elizabeth Baker was granted a license by the Hastings Commissioners to operate two sedan chairs and, in the 1850s, four women owned goods carriers' businesses. One of them, Mrs. Bridget Barton, owned the *Town & Country Carriers*, based at 7 East St. Bridget was born in 1799 and inherited the business on her husband's death sometime around the mid-century. She was summonsed in 1853 after a driver in her employ overloaded three horses. In 1856 Mrs Barton complained to the Council at being charged 1s per load for the beach she carried out of the borough limits. She described herself as a 'very old ratepayer' and suggested that 2d per load would be fairer. The Council decided instead to waive all charges during the summer. Mrs. Barton ran the business into the 1860s. Mary Glyde (b.1821), a widow with three daughters, took over as a fly proprietor[48] on the death of her husband in the early 1860s. (A 'fly' was a quick-travelling, one-horse, covered, lightweight carriage, that is, the mid-19th century equivalent to a taxi-cab.) Unfortunately, in 1867 the fly business, based at 18 Hill Street, went bankrupt but the 1871 Census shows that Mary managed to retain her beer-shop at 4 Hill Street.

The only woman listed as a plumber, glazier and painter was Mary Hall of 19 East Ascent, who appears in the 1862 trades directory.

MAKING & MENDING

Women have traditionally laboured in family workshops, manufacturing a wide range of goods, especially clothing, accessories and domestic items. Some 18th-century craftswomen in Hastings included Widow Smith, who was a periwig maker about 1718, Sarah Holness, who made tobacco-pipes from 1740 to 1769, and Mrs. West, who was a basketmaker in the 1770s.[49] In mid-19th century Hastings, there were women watchmakers and menders,

cabinet makers, chair-makers, chair caners, chair-bottomers, and tobacco pipe trimmers-and-turners.

Clothing manufacture in Hastings was entirely in the hands of small businesses, almost all owned by skilled female dressmakers and milliners, tailors, hatters, glovers, hosiers and shoe- and boot-binders. Women also made underclothing and shirts and a few were embroiderers, furriers, curriers (leather dressers) and feather-workers. During 1834 there was a tailors' strike in Hastings and local needle-women quickly turned their hands to this traditional male skill. When the men returned to work, some of the women failed to revert to their former, ill-paid specialities; indeed, some married tailors and worked alongside them. Making stays and upholstery had also been 'male' preserves; however, by the 1850s, Hastings contained a number of women in these trades.

Needlework was seen as a 'natural' profession for women because it was sedentary and passive, and traditionally performed for the care and maintenance of the family. Where other female workers were thought to develop masculine characteristics the seamstress remained feminine.

Millinery and dressmaking constituted the higher end of female 'needle-employment' and were respectable occupations for women. The number working nationally in this area in the early 1840s was estimated by a House of Commons report to be 15,000. Milliners and dressmakers often came from prosperous working class families who were able to pay for them to be apprenticed. A millinery apprenticeship offered a sense of belonging to a trade, and gave women the opportunity to earn a reasonable living and, perhaps, even the chance to one day run their own business.

Nationally, the skilled millinery and dressmaking trades were damaged by the growing demand for cheap, ready-made clothing. Ready-cut garments (called 'slop-work') were given by employers to less-skilled needlewomen working for very low piece-rates. These slop-workers became a cause célèbre after an 1843 report shocked the public with stories of the cruel exploitation of needlewomen, who lived, worked and died in miserable conditions, often resorting to prostitution to make ends meet.

Thanks to the large number of well-to-do ladies in Hastings & St Leonards, there was plenty of skilled dressmaking work in the towns, particularly in the summer. Upper class ladies dressed to impress and kept their dressmakers very busy creating, altering, mending and ornamenting garments. As it was unthinkable to go outside without a hat or bonnet, manufacturers of headgear also did a roaring trade, selling ready-made items as well as designing and making them to order. There were 249 adult female milliners[50] in Hastings in 1851, making it the second most populous female occupation (after domestic service) and they heavily outnumbered the less-skilled needlewomen. As well as hats and bonnets they made caps, cloaks, mantles, gloves, scarves, muffs, tippets,[51] handkerchiefs, petticoats, hoods and capes. They worked with wool, alpaca, cotton, satin, fur, cambric, lawn, lace, silk and velvet. Upper-crust lady milliners took business trips to Paris and on their return they placed newspaper

James Burton's 1828 plan for the new town of St Leonards intended houses for the poor to be set apart from those of the rich they served. Lavatoria (the washing place) pictured above, and Mercatoria, (for merchants) were even named for their intended occupants. Houses in Lavatoria were fitted with extra-large copper boilers. By 1861, two-thirds of the 18 houses were still occupied by washerwomen.

The public wash-houses in The Bourne, funded by the Countess Waldegrave to encourage hygiene among the poor, were used by Old Town women to perform paid laundry work.

advertisements to advise customers of how *au fait* they were with French fashions, the *dernier cri* in elegance.

In the 1870s, the sewing machine began to come into use in Hastings; a small handful of machinists appears in the 1871 Census, working for dressmakers and tailors.

SOAPSUDS & STRIKES

Laundering has been carried out by poor women for their own families for centuries, and taking in the dirty linen of others turned this domestic skill into a paying trade. In 1851, 236 Hastings women were enumerated as washerwomen, laundresses and mangle-keepers, making this the third most populous female occupation. The work involved heavy and arduous physical labour and fitness and strength were occupational requirements. Some of the newer houses had cold water piped in, but most women had to collect it from a well. Few houses had built-in coal-fired copper boilers, such as were installed in the purpose-built washerwomen's houses known as Lavatoria – 'the washing-place' - in the new town of St Leonards. In the Old Town, linen was boiled in a cauldron hung over a fire and soaping was done in large sinks. There were few labour-saving devices except a wooden 'dolly' with which to work the clothes about and a wash-board for scrubbing. The only detergents were soap and 'elbow grease'. The New Town Act made washerwomen's work a little more troublesome by forbidding laundry to be aired in public places, although items could be spread on the beach to dry. Washed items were passed to mangle-keepers, and thence to professional ironers. Irons were, of course, made of iron and heated on the kitchen range.

As the towns' population grew, commercial laundries opened, employing women to wash and iron, and men to cart and carry. One of the first was owned by Mrs. Ann Tapp, who was in business for at least 20 years until her death in 1854; another belonged to Mary Aldridge, at 87 High Street. While commercial laundries provided more equipment and running water, the volume of work was much greater than women had been accustomed to in their homes. In the second half of the century there was also an increase in the number of clothes worn, especially underclothing, and more curtains and table linen were used.

Laundresses organised the first industrial action by women in Victorian Hastings & St Leonards. In April 1860, there was a brief walkout of commercial washerwomen in one Old Town establishment, possibly Mrs. Aldridge's, over the bad-tempered attitude of a male supervisor. The local paper took a frivolous view of the proceedings:

STRIKE AMONG THE WASHERWOMEN

[T]he hands engaged in a well-known laundry establishment (which has a place and a name not much over one hundred yards from the town clock)[52], and the business of which is visibly - so far as folks out-of-doors know anything about - conducted by one of the sterner sex, who,

Above: Ann Holt was in business with her younger brother from 1838 until 1872.

Below: Ann Walter's advert in the 1850s. Presumably she claimed to be fruiterer and greengrocer 'to the Royal Family' by supplying 57 Marina during Princess Victoria's visit in 1834.

The sex of the proprietor is not evident in either advert and was determined from other sources.

by-the-bye, is the 'don' among the laundry fraternity, as well as the beau ideal of cooks, nursemaids, and other fair damsels who own 'the soft impeachment,' and whose natty 'turn out,' well-kept 'Jerusalem', and polished harness; certainly does credit to this 'antient port,' - suddenly 'struck work' one day last week.

According to 'our own correspondent' this 'nice young laundry-man,' in addition to being rather 'gay,' has also a penchant for John Barleycorn.[53] From one or other cause the 'good lady' of our hero, on the day in question, had a dispute with her liege lord, and the poor 'scrubbers and rubbers' fell in for a share of the bad humour of 'my lord'.

The women could not appreciate these whims, and so with becoming 'spirit' down went soap and soap-suds, soda, blue, and 'stuff' and away went the matrons who generally 'stand at the tub,' and matters - that means the dirty clothes, - and the semi-clean linen remained in status quo (freely translated 'dirty water and wash tub') at the time our informant inspected the 'scene of the disaster.' Whether there was a truce, an importation of 'new hands,' or a satisfactory settlement between master and washerwomen, we know not; but as the glazed hat and blue ribbon, and the quadruped with its necessary 'fixings' were both seen (not the hat, but the owner) doing their usual six miles an hour on Saturday, it is hoped that the clean linen department was attended to with its accustomed regularity.[54]

The inflated style of the press reports accentuates the lowly calling of the washerwomen, mocking them and their concerns, and treats the issue as entertainment. Perhaps this ridicule was preferable to admitting that most of the town was dependent on a group of uneducated women of the labouring classes.

Six months later, prompted by men's campaigns for shorter hours and early-closing days, forty or fifty laundresses and ironers of St Leonards - 'the fair dames of frothy waters and the smoothers of crinoline' - demanded a reduction in hours: their gruelling shifts began at 6am. and finished at 9pm. They wanted to finish at 7pm. instead, or get 6d a day more added to their 2s 6d a day wage, but their employers, most of whom were women, refused. On Monday 3 October the town crier was despatched to let all the town know that the women would work only till Friday, and if their employers did not agree to the reduction in hours, they would walk out. 'This caused quite a commotion throughout the town. Bands of resolute females of all ages hurried from house to house, repeating their demand', recalled Brett, while the _Hastings & St Leonards News_ wrote:

'LESS HOURS OR WE WON'T WORK'

Our township has been the scene of a commotion since the issue of the last impression of the News and it has been a moot point whether clean linen would not be at a premium. The washers and ironers, it appears,

have not yet realized any benefit from the laudable movements which have of late years been gaining ground, for early closing, and shortening the hours of labour of the masculine portion of the labouring population. 'From six in the morning till nine at night' has been 'no fiction' with this hard-worked class. The spirit of disaffection has at length gained the upper hand, and the soap-sudonians, having unsuccessfully demanded 'less work or more pay' - to the extent of two hours' daily abridgment of their toil, or 6d. a day more money - struck work on Friday.

Many of the employers were necessitated to yield to the demands of the toilers, whereat great rejoicing took place. [55]

The employers conceded on the Monday, whereupon the women held a celebration and marched triumphantly carrying a banner behind a hired band:

On Monday evening (having previously primed themselves by potations at the public-houses which they had made their head quarters), they sallied forth through the streets of the district headed by some drums and fifes, and a flag inscribed 'Less hours or we won't work - Britons never shall be slaves.' The scene has been summarized, by those who were on the spot, in the one epithet 'disgraceful.' Under the circumstances perhaps they may be forgiven. It is our sincere desire that these useful personages, having 'won the day,' may make good and beneficial use of the time placed at their disposal. [56]

Brett opined that it was 'generous sympathy which prompted the employers to yield to the demand so readily and so honourably'. He hoped that the women would put the two hours they gained to good use, and suggested the women do 'all in their power to prove by increased interest or activity that the loss to employers it less than they imagine' – in other words, to perform as much work in 13 hours as they had in 15. A correspondent to the *Hastings & St Leonards News* was disappointed that women worked at all:

THE WASHERWOMEN'S HUSBANDS AND PUBLIC HOUSES

I was amused to find, from my wife, that considerable embarrassment had arisen from a strike amongst the washerwomen. Now, I dare say that their hours of labour are long and their wages low, but I would ask the question– Where are the husbands? I am told that many of them earn good wages, as bricklayers, carpenters, &c., who spend their wages (which are now very good), with some few and honourable exceptions, in the public-house. If their wages were applied as they should be, most of these women would be found at home, caring for the house and children. [57]

Unfortunately, he made no suggestion as to who would take care of the town's dirty laundry.

THE MODERN GOVERNESS

A Young Lady's Idea of the Use of Crinoline!

ARTISTES & ARTISANS

Abstracts from the 1851 Census show that 112 Hastings women (compared with only 52 men) were 'engaged in Literature, the Fine Arts, and the Sciences'. On closer inspection however, all but five were schoolmistresses or governesses. The others were three engaged in literature, one in fine art and one in science, with no further details given. There were two actresses and a musician, separately enumerated. Although mid-Victorian Hastings boasted many female poets, authors, painters and sketchers, almost without exception these were middle-class accomplishments and not paid occupations. Bessie Rayner Parkes[58] for example was a published writer whose books were reviewed in Hastings' local press, yet the 1851 Census shows her as 'unoccupied'. Twenty years later things had changed to the extent that middle class ladies such as artist Joanna Samworth of Brooklands Cottage, Mary Howard of 47 Wellington Square, a writer of theology and topography and novelist Mary Pulloyne of Cambridge Terrace were enumerated as professionals in the arts.

Some women made a living from handicrafts, such as Shell Artistes and French Paper-Flower Makers. In 1861, spinster Sarah Parkes was the first Hastings woman to work with the new technology of cameras, as an 'artist & photographist' in Robertson Street. Ten years later, Elizabeth Gillard was an 'assistant photographist & painter', Florence Parker was an 'assistant to photographer', Sarah Welton was a 'photographic artist' and Lucy Godbold of 8 Grand Parade was a 'photographic painter'. Her father was a well-known photographer and she had probably been his apprentice.

Throughout the century, many touring performers stayed in Hastings for a season, including actresses and singers, and Mrs. Wombwell brought her famous travelling Menagerie more than once. For a season in 1872, Miss Sarah Thorne was granted a theatrical license for the Market Hall, wherein she played Lady Macbeth.

Most unusually, Emma Hume was organist at St Mary Magdalen Church from its opening in 1859 until her marriage in 1864. She will not have received any payment for this and probably was appointed because she was the rector's daughter. Emma trained a choir and gave concerts; one performance attracted an audience of 300. She played at society weddings, including that of an MP's daughter in 1862. The church had opened with a secondhand organ and, in her honour, a fund was opened on her wedding day to purchase a new one.[59] Two blind girl organists, Ellen (13) and Emily (17) and their brother Tommy (11) gave a recital at St Mary-in-the-Castle in 1856. Brett reported that, 'Their performance, separately, of five pieces each astonished and delighted all the large number of persons present'.[60]

SCHOOLS & SEMINARIES

Because all other professions were closed to them, for intelligent women with ambition, teaching was the closest thing to a career in public service and was the only academic career available. Somehow rising above their own meagre education, by 1841, there were over 29,000 schoolmistresses in Britain. Hundreds of women in mid-19th century Hastings followed this occupation. Some worked in Sunday schools, national schools and endowed schools but many more owned, managed and taught in dozens of private seminaries. The majority of schoolmistresses in Hastings were not born there; a good many came from London, and beyond.

For mid-Victorian feminists, education was the key to women's emancipation. Firstly, educating women fitted them to become teachers, thus providing careers for thousands of spinsters and widows. Secondly, educated women would become aware of their subordinate position and join the feminist cause. Thirdly, educated women would be living proof that women had the intellect to enter the professions and would confirm that women were fit to have the vote. Lastly, it was hoped that these independent career women would act as examples to the younger generation of women. Teaching was, therefore, a hotbed of feminism and it comes as no surprise that the first women's suffrage society in Hastings was founded by the proprietor of a ladies seminary.

Prior to the advent of a national education system, all schools were privately owned. Women owned and ran many private seminaries, both day and boarding. Two proprietors in Hastings in 1817 were Mrs. Kelly, High Street and Mrs. Richards, All Saints' Street. In the 1830s Mrs. Bray opened a school at Blucher Buildings[61] which later moved to 2 Wellington Place. Miss Lydia Borrow (b. 1790) ran a school at 117 High Street from 1837 until 1874, assisted by her younger sister, Martha. She began by taking in her brother's five children when their mother died. One, George Borrow, was later to be a fairly well-known author and sea-painter. As the century progressed seminaries became numerous and the Censuses show that children were sent from all over the world to be educated here.

Only one of the two endowed schools in Hastings employed mistresses. James Saunders died in 1708, leaving money to support a school for boys and two mixed infants' schools each taking 30 children. The latter were run by 'school-dames', who were paid £10 a year – a housemaid's wage - compared to £40 paid to the boys' schoolmasters. As there was so little employment for educated middle class women there was no shortage of applicants, even at such a low salary. An advert in 1811 drew six candidates, a large number considering the town's tiny population. Later the salary was raised to £25 but from this they had to pay for the rent and coals of the school-room.

FINISHING GOVERNESS.

A LADY is desirous of obtaining for a young friend, at present visiting in her house, a situation as Resident and Finishing Governess in a Nobleman's or Gentleman's Family. She is a first-rate musician, and speaks French, acquired in Paris, with fluency and great purity of accent. She has lately quitted a Nobleman's Family, where she resided two years, from whom, as well as from other friends, she can have high testimonials.

Address, A. B. C., 35, Wellington square, Hastings.

HOME EDUCATION.

THE MISSES NICKOLLS receive a select and limited number of Young Ladies to Board and Educate; their desire is to impart a solid and Religious Education, based on strictly Church of England principles. The Establishment is conducted like that of a private family. The Misses Nickolls beg to inform parents who are wishing their children to enjoy a lengthened residence at Hastings for the benefit of the Sea Air, &c., that they may depend upon every attention being rendered to the health and happiness of those committed to their care.

Terms known on application; the quarter to commence from the time of entering.

Text taken from a board found in St Clement's Church.

The national education system began when members of the Church of England became concerned that working-class children couldn't read the Bible. In 1811 the National Society for Promoting the Education of the Poor in the Principles of the Established Church was formed. This provided Sunday schools, then weekday schools which, from 1839, were subsidised.

Elementary education wasn't compulsory until 1880, but from 1862 the government set standards for pupils in subsidised schools requiring all children to be able to read and write simple paragraphs and to do arithmetic; in addition, girls had to learn needlework.

The first Sunday school in Hastings was opened by a lady in 1812 and was attached to All Saints' Church. The first in St Leonards was founded by a group of ladies headed by Mrs. Elizabeth Burton, at 36 Marina, before 1830.[62] This grew and was moved into a corner of the Assembly Rooms, then to some low buildings at St Clement's Place, East Ascent, with Mr. & Mrs. Tebay in charge. It later merged with the St Leonards National and Parochial School that opened in Mercatoria in 1847. The first master and mistress of this national school were from the north of England. Mr. Gibson was paid £60 a year while his wife received £45. Their house was rent-free. It is interesting that Mrs. Gibson continued as the school's mistress while raising a family.

The first day-school in Hastings was Cavendish Place Infants' which was established in 1829 by the Infant School Society and funded chiefly by Countess Waldegrave. Mistresses Martha and Amelia Andrew worked from 8 until 6 in the summer and until 4 in the winter. They had to collect two-penny fees from each child on Monday mornings. The first church day school in Hastings was the Parochial Boys', Girls' and Infants', founded by the minister of St Mary-in-the-Castle in 1830, and given a proper schoolroom by Mrs. Vores, wife of the rector, at Portland Place in 1848. [63]

Hastings Union.—SCHOOLMISTRESS WANTED.

NOTICE IS HEREBY GIVEN, that the Board of Guardians of the Hastings Union will, at their meeting, which will be held at the Board Room of the Hastings Workhouse, on Thursday, the 20th of October instant, proceed to elect a single person, not exceeding forty years of age, to fill the situation of Schoolmistress to the Hastings Workhouse. Salary £20 per annum, with board and residence in the house.

The person to be appointed must be accustomed to the National School system of education, and she will be required to instruct the children in knitting, sewing, mending clothes, &c., and to enter upon the duties of the office on the 27th day of October instant.

Written applications, accompanied by testimonials, are to be forwarded, free of expense, to the Hastings Workhouse, on or before Wednesday, the 19th day of October instant, addressed "To the Chairman of the Board of Guardians of the Hastings Union," and the Board would prefer the personal attendance of the respective applicants at their meeting on the next day (Thursday), at two o'clock in the afternoon.

By order of the Guardians,

Hastings, October 6, 1853.　　　F. C. INSKIPP, Clerk.

National Schools, founded and run by the Church of England, and British Schools, owned by the nonconformist churches, followed by the introduction of compulsory universal schooling in 1870, revolutionised women's employment possibilities. From the 1830s, parishes began to open schools, providing many thousands of careers for educated and ambitious women. In these schools, women could teach only infants and girls. This was mainly because women had insufficient qualifications to teach the boys' curriculum, since they were denied entry to all universities. However, once women became entrenched in the national education system, the need for them to be properly qualified was a very persuasive factor in the campaign to open universities to women. Frequently, a teacher taught monitors, who taught the children. This developed into the pupil-teacher system in which children were apprenticed to a teacher, after which they could take an exam for college. After training college, they could get a certificate allowing them to teach.

The first British girls' school in Hastings was opened, under the patronage of the Duchess of Kent, at a Wesleyan Chapel in Waterloo Place in 1835. It had places for 100 girls.[64] St Clement's and All Saints' National Schools also opened in 1835 with fees of a penny a week per child. The girls' section, 200-strong, moved to 99-100 All Saints' Street in 1853. One of the early head monitors of this school, Mary Ann Pickerden, became a fully-qualified and certificated teacher, whereupon she left Hastings to work in Birmingham. In 1863 Maria Caldwell became the seventh mistress from the school to compete for a Scholarship and to be elected a Queen's Scholar of the First Class. Her prize was one year's instruction with board, lodging, laundry, medical attendance and £3 spending money. (Male winners of the same prize received £4.) In the 1850s and 60s, National Schools sprung up at St Mary Magdalen, Magdalen Road; Christchurch, Alfred Street[65] (under Miss T. Moon); Hollington (Mrs Mary Harmer); and Halton.

Because of the monitorial system, some very young girls are enumerated in the Census as pupil teachers; the youngest discovered was just 13.

The Hastings Union Workhouse contained a small school, with a master and mistress. In 1847 Elizabeth Tebay[66] was suspended and later dismissed for being drunk while taking the children out for exercise. The Governor's daughter, Emily Harman, took charge of the children temporarily and although the vacancy was advertised in the local paper, she was appointed. In 1851 she was highly praised by the Government Inspector of Schools and was presented with a gift. She must have left by 1853, since the Union re-advertised the position. In 1867, Miss Sarah Pusey was mistress, at a salary of £50 per annum plus board.

The School of Industry at Albion House (later 15 Priory Road) was established by heiress Miss Sayer in 1847. Seventeen girls were admitted, fed, clothed and instructed in 'the duties and employment of domestic servants'. The Ragged School Union, founded in 1844, opened schools for children whose ragged clothing was not acceptable to the church schools. The first in Hastings was opened in 1855 in Stone Street, and later one was opened by Miss Margaret Paton in a former church hall at 39a Tackleway.

ALBERT HOUSE, Cross-street, Warrior-square.—Industrial and invalid kitchen, for supplying tickets to the sick and infirm poor, for meat, puddings, &c., and for instructing girls in kitchen and household work. Emma Baker, Superintendent.

Emma Baker, a married woman with a small child, was nevertheless in charge of the soup kitchen and servants' training school at Cross St, since demolished and now the site of a new housing development. Her husband was butler at one of the grand houses in Warrior Square.

Hastings Infirmary, now the site of White Rock Theatre. Workplace of many Matrons and nurses.

By 1862 the number of children grew too large for the hall and a fundraising bazaar earned £500 for new premises.

The largest and finest seat of learning for girls was All Souls' Convent, which had opened in 1834 as a nunnery. By 1871 it was the most cosmopolitan building in the area. Mother Superior Cornelia Connelly of Philadelphia USA and her two assistants headed an impressive array of 20 female teachers from as far afield as Lancashire, Devon, Ireland, Switzerland and Italy. They were all specialists in their subjects, which included music, singing, painting, literature, Latin, French, German, grammar, drawing and needlework. There were 91 girls boarding at the school in 1871, aged from eight to 25. They hailed from London, York, Warwick, Ireland, the USA, India, Australia, Venezuela and St Lucia. The establishment had 35 live-in servants, of whom 32 were female, including a doorkeeper, a dairymaid and a baker. The youngest servant was aged eight: she was the 'second-under-kitchen-maid-in-training'.

Educated and enterprising women also offered private tuition in their own homes, in music, singing, dancing, drawing and languages – generally, French. They were usually described as 'Professors' but this was merely a courtesy title with no academic substantiation.

A list of female school proprietors and private tutors from 1817 to 1854 can be found in the Appendix.

MATRONS & MANAGERS

Women were employed by churches, charities, public institutions and services, but rarely was any woman placed in even the lowest ranks of power or influence, and never was she placed in authority over men, except manservants. The highest a woman could hope for was to obtain a post as a matron and, to be considered, an applicant had to be respectable, pious and of unblemished reputation. There was such a lack of career or promotional opportunities for women that they tended to retain good situations for as long as possible.

Within the church, a woman could be a deaconess, nun or an Anglican sister, The 1851 Census abstracts show two women 'church officers'; these were probably pew-openers, a traditional women's job in the church. They were usually widows, who worked most of Sunday, spent much of Saturday polishing the pews and attended on weekdays for weddings and funerals. Coins received from the congregation amounted to about 30s per year. Presumably the church gave pew-openers free accommodation, since the 'salary' was about 1/7th of the average woman's wage. Despite that, 'A Cambridge Graduate' complained in a letter to the local press about having to give a penny to the pew opener at St. Clement's Church. Other religious workers mentioned in Censuses include Lucy Smith, chapel-keeper at the Congregational Church at Robertson Street in 1861 and Ann McCarthur, born in Gibraltar and living at 2 Pelham Street, whose occupation was given as 'Missionary for Hastings'. Elizabeth Mackie of 15 Stone Street was listed as a 'biblewoman' in 1871.

A rather unkind contemporary depiction of a nosy 1840s postmistress, peeping into someone's mail.

2 Church Passage, once the home of Hannah Goodwin (1798-1854) who in 1828 became Matron in charge of St-Mary-in-the-Castle Poorhouse and was later a pew-opener at St Clement's Church. The cottage is now a Grade II listed building.

Working women were hampered by the voluminous skirts typical of the mid-19th century.

Gaols, lockups, poorhouses and workhouses employed women as matrons and attendants. These posts were often held by wives of the institution's governor and on his death, his widow was, on occasion, allowed to take over. Ivy Pinchbeck[67] records that certain parishes in 18th century Hertfordshire recognised the right of a widow to succeed her late husband as a gaol-keeper, and the 1841 Census shows that 1,598 British women were 'Keeper, or Head of Public Institution'. Almost without exception, such a job would not, however, be open to new female applicants.

In Hastings in 1753, Sally Lovekin and her husband were appointed Master and Matron of St Clement's Poorhouse (known as *The Pilchard*) in George Street. [68] When he died in 1760 she became Governor pro. tem., assisted by her daughter. A public meeting voted by 34 votes to six that she should continue, and she held the post for five years.[69] St Mary-in-the-Castle Poorhouse was governed by a woman for nine years. Hannah Goodwin (née Easton) was born in 1798 and by the age of 24 was a destitute widow with three children, the youngest just 12 months old. After working as a monthly nurse, in 1828 she took charge of the poorhouse, located at what is now 12-16 Wellington Place. When it closed in 1837 - the workhouse took over its role - she lost her job. In 1848 she became a pew-opener and, with her dressmaker daughter, moved into 2 Church Passage, a cottage adjoining a grave yard, comprising three rooms and a wash-house. Her sight failed and she became unable to work. She died in 1854.

At the small gaol at The Bourne[70] a Matron superintended the female prisoners and did the housekeeping. As living quarters were shared, the Matron was of necessity the wife of the Master.[71] For this reason, the Hastings Gaol Matron's post was not advertised; however, an advertisement for a Gaol Matron at Petworth in 1852 required 'a person not less than 30, nor more than 45 years, at a salary of £50 per annum, with coals and candles in addition, but no rations'.

In Hastings magistrates' reports, several women's names appear as 'female searchers'; all were the wives of police officers or gaolers. Most probably they were drafted in by their husbands on an informal, ad-hoc basis to search suspects. A small gratuity may have been given them, although it may have been an accepted duty of any woman marrying a man employed in the lower ranks of law enforcement.

Women were Superintendents and Matrons at a wide range of charitable institutions, including Ladies' Homes, Servants' Homes, Convalescent Homes, Industrial Kitchens and Mendicity Houses. The first Matron of White Rock Infirmary, opened in 1841, was Mrs. Crouch, whose initial weekly wage of 8s was soon raised to 12s, plus free accommodation, coals and wood. She was succeeded by Miss Griffen, former housekeeper at the Foundling Hospital, London, who was selected from 22 applicants in 1862. Frances Hartley soon replaced her and remained in that post for 20 years, retiring only because of her defective vision. Similar longevity was demonstrated by Maria Marshall, who was Matron of West Hill Industrial School for 22 years until her death.

In 1871, Mary Pank, a widow aged 54, was 'Superintendent of the Insane' at a private asylum at 76 Marina, where she supervised two male

I say, Sally, wot a good thing it would be if ve vos to jine your £100 wot the Old Man left yer and the £30 you've got in the Savings Bank & the £10 a year wot Missis left yer and them ere 5 Sovereigns wot young Master guv yer, to my *seven shillings & sixpence* a veek & the Christmas Box wot Master's a going to give me - ve might then open a Beer shop!

Cartoon by Charles Dickens. Published by W Spooner 377 Strand, London.

The footman approaches the cook with a very appealing offer: if they combine their assets, they might escape domestic service and gain liberty and independence through opening a beer-shop.

attendants and a housemaid. In her charge were four male 'lunatics' two of whom were Lords.

A Postmaster was a servant of the Crown, and was usually assisted by his wife or daughter. Postmistresses were common all over the UK and appear in directories for several Sussex towns. The first woman employee at Hastings Post Office was Mrs. West. In 1824 her Postmaster husband George was dismissed and, when a relative took over, Mrs. West was retained as assistant. The Post Office was then at 53 High Street, giving Post Office Passage its name. Mr. Bond took over in 1829 and moved it to 55 High Street. He was dismissed in 1831 and his daughter Alicia became Postmaster, receiving the same salary: £62 a year plus emoluments worth £81. She retained the job for two years.[72] In the 1850s, Post Office Receiving Houses were located at Mrs. Ann Gallopp's shop at 6 St Mary's Terrace and at Mrs. Osborne's at 27 Castle Street. In 1867, Elizabeth Blackman was proprietress of the 'Post & Money Order Office' at Ore.

The 1851 Census abstracts show three Hastings women 'employed by Local Government' but a search of the actual Census has failed to find them.

FISHWIVES & FISHMONGERS

Hastings' ancient fishing fleet was still central to the economy of the town in the mid-century, when 500 families were engaged in the fishery. In 1850 there were 88 boats and by 1861 this had increased to 150. Some women, for example Charlotte Clarke, owned a fishing boat. Although the 1841 Census abstracts list 306 'fisherwomen' in Britain, none of them was in Hastings; however, women and girls did work in the industry helping husbands, fathers or sons by mending nets, and by cleaning and gutting fish and preparing them for sale. Census enumerators listed them as 'fisherman's wives' and did not record this work unless the woman herself owned a fishmonger business separately from her husband's employment. There were several women fishmongers in the town, and when the new fishmarket opened in 1870, the 12 stallholders comprised four women, six men, and two whose gender is not recorded. Women also hawked fish and shrimps from barrows and baskets in streets and public houses.

Fishermen's families lived, as they had for centuries, in circumstances of chronic insolvency but they constituted a cohesive community of many interconnected and extended families. Although it seemed chaotic, life in the fishery was structured by 'rhythms of poverty' caused by the weekly and seasonal fluctuations in income. The mid-1800s were, overall, prosperous years for Hastings fisherfolk, but there were many dips in their fortunes and it fell to wives to ensure that their families did not starve. Most had a means of earning money when they needed to: performing laundry, sewing, charring and baby-minding. Steve Peak relates how, in 1858, some local gentlemen put forth a plan to set up a local net-making business, to give employment to women, elderly fishermen and boys. However, the plan was abandoned because they would not accept the

SERVANT GIRLS.

To the Editor of "The Hastings and St. Leonards News."

Sir,—I feel it to be my duty not to withhold the information given on the authority of the police, that "on Sunday the public-houses are filled with servant girls who are sent by their mistresses to church."

Can anything be done to put an end to this scandalous disobedience and deceit? One cannot wonder that it should lead to vice and crime, as seen in the melancholy case of depravity brought before the magistrates of Hastings last week. Servants, in these days, are a source of deep anxiety and discomfort to their employers, and I hesitate not to say that their state generally has become one of the crying evils of the age, and demands the earnest consideration of every thinking mind.

The first step towards grappling with an evil is to *know* it. The general character of Hastings servants, and of the St. Mary's terrace girls in particular, is disgracefully bad; and some whom I could name are a nuisance to the neighbourhood. Of course there are exceptions, and those masters and mistresses who are well and faithfully served cannot be too thankful. I have suffered deeply; but I shall not have suffered in vain if the injury and loss inflicted upon me should lead to the mitigation, in any degree, of the evils now existing.

I am, sir, yours truly,

ELIZABETH COOPER.

Coppenhall Rectory, Crewe, Cheshire,
  September 10th, 1866.

low wages necessary to make them competitive, and the nets instead continued to be made at Bridport. Peak remarks that Old Town women could make more money charring and taking in washing. [73]

The Countess of Waldegrave inadvertently helped fishwives in these money-making activities when she paid £2,000 to build public wash-houses in Bourne Street in 1865, with the intention of improving the level of cleanliness and hygiene of the poor – 'the great unwashed'. For a small fee, the women used the laundry facilities to carry out their usual work of washing, drying and ironing other people's clothes.

An aspect of life that made fishermen's wives staunch allies and set them apart from other women was the danger their husbands faced every day. In the 1860s, during an 8½ -year period, 24 Hastings fishermen were lost at sea. One widow was left with seven children to support and one more on the way. For each tragedy a subscription fund was opened, to which the Mayor, the Countess Waldegrave, Frederick North and other dignitaries contributed. The total collected for the 24 families was £1257. [74]

Every September, hundreds of Old Town women took a 'working holiday': they earned money for the winter by hop-picking in the fields on the outskirts of Hastings, taking along with them many children.

SERVANTS & SKIVVIES

The overwhelming majority of working class girls entered domestic service, which was the largest category of occupation for women throughout the 19th century. There were 1,100 of them in Hastings in 1851 – over 36% of all self-supporting women. Censuses show some as young as eight and nine.

A related job was that of charwoman, a skivvy employed on a daily basis in commercial and industrial premises. This was generally the province of desperate older women, particularly widows, who had only domestic skills to offer to an employer. In the 1860s, newly-widowed Ann Russell of 1, Lavatoria worked as a charwoman to support five small children (the youngest was aged one month), as well as her mother-in-law who lived in as childminder.

Domestic service seemed to be the answer to everybody's needs. People wanted servants, and women needed work. Little training was required and, as an added bonus, the work fitted girls to become wives. The only fly in the ointment was that most girls would have preferred to be doing just about anything else. In 1864 one reluctant servant, 16-year-old Fanny Beaton, made her feelings known rather spectacularly, by twice setting fire to her bed, which was located in the kitchen and was fully-enclosed with wooden shutters. Fanny admitted that her mistress, Mary Akehurst of 12 Marine Parade, was kind to her; she had simply wanted to go home. She was sent to prison for one month. [75]

In a small middle-class or prosperous working-class household, one maid-of-all-work was engaged to carry out the most menial chores, often as an assistant to the housewife. The pay was about 2s a week plus board for a

Few houses had piped water, so fetching it from the well was a daily task common to domestic servants.

6½-day week which began about 6am and finished at 10 or 11pm. It was not unusual for servants to share a small attic-room and, in some cases, even the same bed, while others slept in kitchens situated in damp basements. Their few personal possessions were stored in a small trunk known as their 'box'. As the family's income rose, so did the number of servants, and this served as an outward sign of prosperity. In a medium-sized house, a parlourmaid and cook would be engaged as well. Only the largest, grandest households employed higher servants such as a lady's maid, butler or footman.

A woman with refined manners and pleasant conversation might find employment as a personal companion. One in Hastings was Judith Dickinson, a 'Company Keeper' to a 72-year-old lady in the 1850s. Likewise, a genteel lady fallen on hard times, if she had a little education and refinement, could become a children's governess, of which there were 44 in Hastings in 1851. They were socially isolated: too high-class to mix with the lower servants; too low-class to be friends of their employers. Bessie Rayner Parkes[76] said in 1859 that 'no class of men can compete with the governess in wretchedness' because they were so ill-paid and ill-used, and could never earn enough to put anything aside for their old age. Specialist charities were unable to cope with the sheer number of distressed, even destitute, former governesses.

The austere life of servants was thrown into sharp contrast by their wealthy employers' array of beautiful clothes and accessories. A servant could never afford to buy such things for herself. Pilfering from employers was common; many girl servants were prosecuted and custodial sentences were the norm. Honest girls, who purchased cheap imitations - paste jewellery, pretty hair-slides, a bit of lace or perhaps a gay straw hat - were roundly criticised for their 'love of finery'. It was even described as a 'social evil' by the editor of the *Hastings & St Leonards News*, who condemned servant girls for loving 'tawdry finery' and blamed their 'ignorant mothers' for fostering in them a 'love of "showing off" beyond their station'. He believed that 'a lady is perfectly justified in forbidding her domestic to dress in a style which is plainly beyond her honest means' and advised that she 'refuse to allow her to appear in public in the guise of a poppet or with the airs of a fool'. He suggested that the reason these 'silly girls' dressed up was 'to get the power of dazzling butcher's boys', which meant that they were 'graduating for a life of sin or a home of misery'. In conclusion, he reminded readers that there was 'Christian work' for 'kindhearted' women in saving these 'poor creatures' from the 'ruinous consequences of a giddy love of dress which too surely await so many of these victims of bad taste and ignorance'.[77]

The fabulously wealthy Countess of Waldegrave echoed these sentiments in 1867 when she gave a stern lecture to schoolgirls on the merits of saving up their surplus pennies to purchase warm clothes for winter, instead of indulging their love of finery. She warned that, when (not if) they became servants, their mistresses would disapprove of their attempts to get above their station in life. God was cited in support: He, in His wisdom, had

This Indenture witnesseth that *Mary Ann Stace* aged fourteen years and eight months or thereabouts by and with the consent of her brother *George Stace* of *No 2 Castle Street* ... doth put herself Apprentice to *John Henry* and *Thomas Pycroft* of *Nos 8 & 9 Breeds Place* ...to learn their Art and with them after the manner of an Apprentice to serve from the 31st day of December one thousand Eight hundred and sixty-seven.

Unto the full End and Term of two Years from thence next following to be following to be fully complete and ended. During the said Term the said Apprentice her Masters faithfully shall serve their secrets keep their lawful commands everywhere gladly do she shall do no damage to her said Masters nor see to be done of others but to her power she shall tell or forthwith give warning to her said Masters of the same. She shall not waste the Goods of her said Masters nor lend them lawfully to any she shall not commit fornication nor contract Matrimony within the said Term. She shall not play at Cards or at Dice Table nor at any other unlawful games whereby her said Masters may have any loss with their own goods or others during the said Term without the license of her said Masters. She shall neither buy nor sell she shall not haunt Taverns or Playhouses nor absent herself from her said Masters service day or night unlawfully but in all things as a faithful Apprentice she shall behave herself towards her said Masters and all theirs during the said Term.

And the said *John Henry* and *Thomas Pycroft* masters in consideration of the services of said Apprentice in the Art or trade of Draper which he useth by the best means he can shall teach or Instruct or cause to be taught and instructed Finding unto the said Apprentice sufficient Meat, Drink, lodging and all other Necessaries during said Term.

The wording of Mary Ann Stace's apprenticeship indenture. Reproduced by courtesy of Hastings Museums and Art Gallery.

allotted to each her correct place in society. To contradict His plan was blasphemous.

Mr. J Tanner of 30 All Saints' Street opened a room in his house as a registry office, so that girls who had newly arrived in town could obtain places as servants as soon as possible, 'that the evils of idleness night be avoided'. He charged nothing, but later commercial agencies were opened - the forerunners of today's employment agencies.

ASSISTANTS & APPRENTICES

While towns in other parts of Britain had large factories and textile mills, mid-Victorian Hastings had no single large employer of women; only commercial laundries and the major hotels engaged more than a handful of female staff. Most women employed commercially worked in small shops and workshops, laundries and catering establishments.

In the clothing trades, employment for journeywomen (day-workers) was not lucrative; indeed, needlewomen were something of a cause célèbre in the national press during the 1840s. Their hours were excessively long and the work unhealthy. In 1862 a lady journalist warned, 'all who are wise will avoid this profession ... because such numbers crowd into it, that the competition drives the payment down to a point below that at which life can be sustained'.[78]

Few women were employed as shop assistants outside of their own families prior to the 1860s, when they began to work in bakery, confectionery, drapery and millinery shops. Some were apparently taken on without wages, at least at first. For example, Miss Frost was 'in service to' draper William Bowerman in Robertson Street for seven months in 1872 without pay. Extracts from a diary of a milliner's shop-girl in Hastings in the 1860s show that her typical working day began at 8 or 9am and ended between 7 and 10pm. Saturday hours were usually the longest. There was early closing on Wednesday, when she finished at 5pm.[79] Early closing in Hastings had its origins in an 1850s campaign for provision shops to close early on Saturdays - at 9pm instead of the customary time of between 10 and midnight. This was born of concern that employees may be too tired for 'the religious duties of the Sabbath morning.'[80]

Some girls managed to secure apprenticeships in small workshops. Millinery required an apprenticeship of up to seven years and it was a father's decision whether to pay for his daughter. Most, it seems, would not: a mere three girls' names appear among a long list of apprentices in Hastings between 1710-52, for example. By the 1850s there were many more, apprenticed to both women and men. Emily and Harriet Barrow took on three millinery apprentices in their business at Havelock Road. Apprentices received no wages.

In hotels, eating houses, coffee shops and pubs, girls and women worked as waitresses, cooks, barmaids and chambermaids. The Census lists barmaids as young as 15. The *Royal Victoria Hotel* employed and housed 12

John Leech's depiction of idle domestic servants. 1869.

female staff in 1871 while at the *Queen's Hotel* there were 20. Few women were employed as managers. One of the first was Mrs. Raven, cook and manager at the *Horse & Groom*, Mercatoria, in the 1830s.[81] Miss Bowles was manager of the *Albion Hotel* in the late 1860s and, in the 1870s, Emma Gribble was shop manager of a cook and confectionery business at 5 Marina Colonnade. The 1871 Census shows that Sarah Ellis, a lady from Cambridge, was assistant manager of the prestigious *Seaside Hotel*, Stratford Place.

Until the late-19th century, all office work was considered the domain of men. The pioneer female clerks in Hastings were book-keepers. The 1861 Census shows that Ann Wells worked for James Emary at the *Albion Hotel*, and Ellen Waghorne worked for her uncle, a butcher, at 14 Castle Street. In 1871 Mary Hunt was book-keeper at the *Queen's Hotel*.

Almost every young working woman was housed by her employer, who could thus keep a watchful eye on her behaviour at all times. Also, domestics could double as shop assistants and vice versa. With no minimum wage and no trades unions, the pay was usually too low to afford lodgings. Furthermore, many working girls were young teenagers, for whom it was not respectable to live independently and 'unprotected'.

HAWKERS & HARLOTS

[Women who are] a step from starvation ... "must try the streets," as they will describe it. If they are young and reckless, they become prostitutes; if in more advanced years, or with good principles, they turn street-sellers; but this is only when destitution presses sharply'.

Henry Mayhew.[82]

Mayhew's observation about London was true of Hastings. The lowest and most desperate occupations in town took place on the streets. Beggars will be dealt with in *Down & Out in Victorian Hastings* (forthcoming) and will not, therefore, be included in this section.

Hawkers

All kinds of food was hawked until 1832, when Hastings Commissioners passed a Local Act that allowed only fish to be hawked in the streets and which levied market tolls on other foodstuffs, ranging from 1s 6d a day for meats down to a 1d for butter, which made it more difficult for women to afford to run a stall. Consequently, they turned to street-hawking, and hawkers both old and new turned to selling wool-work, bead-work, crochet-work, shell-work, stay-laces, baskets, flowers, cottons, combs, toys, lace, buttons and matches. They would buy or make a small number of cheap items and walk the streets, usually for more than 12 hours a day, trying to sell them. Policemen and magistrates regarded hawking as a mere front for begging. They wanted the town 'tidied up' of these scruffy, pestilential persons who annoyed the genteel visitor and thus threatened the town's tourism industry. Their solution was to raise the price of a hawker's license *tenfold*. This placed it beyond the means of the poorest and those who operated without a license were thus criminalised, prosecuted, fined and even imprisoned. It was a cruel blow against people who had hit rock bottom but were still trying to support themselves. In addition, shop-owning tradesmen campaigned against hawkers. In 1860, 40 of them sent a petition to the council complaining about the increase in street-selling. Hawking was made so difficult that it is probable that some women pushed out of the work added themselves to the growing ranks of Hastings' prostitutes.

Hawkers were often very brash and colourful characters. As no-one employed them, they did not need to maintain a genteel or humble demeanour but would brazenly call out their wares. During their arduous day they frequented beer shops for much-needed refreshment and were frequently the worse for drink. One, Fanny Dunstall, was prosecuted for 'being drunk and furiously driving her horse and cart to the danger of foot passengers' in Robertson Street in 1862. She was fined 10s plus 4s 4d costs.

Harlots

Prostitution was rife in Victorian England. The cream of the trade lived like ladies in fine houses and were discreetly 'kept' by 'gentleman friends', but working-class prostitution took place in public or in squalid rented rooms. It was resorted to out of desperation and was often of a temporary nature. It was well-known for example that sometimes needle-women were forced into occasional, clandestine prostitution when business was slow; they later married, or the work picked up and, with luck, no-one found out.

Others were not so fortunate. Without the safety-net of a welfare system, a typical scenario was that a girl who was illiterate, abandoned, alcoholic, orphaned, or too weak for domestic service, found refuge as the 'unmarried wife' of a man prepared, initially, to support her. Before long something usually went awry: the 'husband' put her on the streets, or the relationship ended, leaving the woman destitute and with a 'past'. Other women lost their reputations by having illegitimate children. In all these cases the woman, in the parlance of the day, was 'ruined' - that is, no longer a virgin and, having nothing left to lose, became a prostitute.

The first prostitutes recorded in 19th-century Hastings were Lucy Ballard in 1820 and Sarah Mitchell in 1826 who were arrested, apparently, simply for 'wandering in the streets'. By mid-century there were dozens operating in the town and the same women appeared in front of magistrates time and time again, among them Portsmouth Poll, Dover Lizzy, Mary Ann Wratten, Elizabeth Watts and the notorious Mary Keene, who was reputed to have been cautioned by every policeman in the Hastings force.

A range of euphemisms was used to describe them: 'members of the frail sisterhood', 'frail and fair ones', 'girls of the town', 'nymphs of the pave', 'our incorrigibles', 'ladies of certain lax morals' or, most commonly, 'unfortunates'. In 1871 one magistrate publicly labelled Sarah Eldridge a 'social pest'. Coventry Patmore, a one time Hastings resident, saw them as degrading something beautiful:

> Ah, wasteful woman, she who may
> On her sweet self set her own price
> Knowing man cannot choose but pay
> How has she cheapen'd paradise. [83]

Most of them ended up in a terribly degraded condition, plying a trade of the most sordid description in the dismal back-yards and alleyways of the Old Town at 6d a time. Prostitution centred on Hastings' numerous disreputable public houses and beer shops; indeed, any flashy single woman swilling alcohol at the bar of such a place was sure to be a 'fallen one'. At first, alcohol numbed the shame and overcame the inhibitions of girls new to the trade but, all too swiftly, drunkenness became a way of life and many drank themselves into oblivion every day. After being 'treated' to a few penny shots of gin, they would totter along the gas-lit streets describing to passing men, in terms of the basest vulgarity, what was on offer. If a policeman heard them, or a man complained, they were charged with 'being drunk and using obscene language', to avoid a charge of soliciting, which would require the accosted gentlemen to attend court.

Prostitutes increased publicans' profits and many a blind eye was turned as they solicited for trade on the premises. However, it was an offence for a publican to 'allow persons of notorious bad character to assemble'. Such was the oft-repeated charge against several licensees in the 1850s, among them Richard Wood, landlord of the *Privateer*, Wellington Mews, who was reported by Sergeant Brazier for allowing 'fiddling and dancing' in his pub after midnight, and for permitting two known prostitutes, 'Dover Lizzy' and 'Sally Bates', and two other girls to 'carouse' with young men. Wood, as a repeat offender, was fined 10s plus 15s 5d costs.[84] William Huggett was summoned for 'allowing prostitutes and persons of notorious bad character to assemble' at his pub the *Ship*, in Bourne Street. One night Inspector Battersby found twelve to fourteen men with four prostitutes in a back room. Two days later he found a man in the pub's backyard 'in a very indecent position with a drunken prostitute.' He halted their congress, but later returned to find 'the same pair engaged in the same act in the same place'. He remarked to magistrates, 'I consider it to be a worse place than a common brothel'. Mr. Huggett was fined 10s and 19s 6d costs.[85]

The landlord of the *Queen's Head* (a fishermen's pub) was luckier. When renewing his licence, magistrates heard that he habitually harboured prostitutes but, as he had never been convicted, the renewal was granted. The landlord of the *Duke of York*, Union Road, St Leonards, was not so fortunate; he lost his home and his livelihood. At midnight one Monday in August 1864, a policeman's attention was drawn to the pub by the sound of music and singing. Inside he found 13 men carousing with six women, five of

THE GREAT SOCIAL EVIL.

Above A cartoon from the 1860s depicting prostitutes standing in the rain awaiting customers. *Below* one of the alleyways of the Old Town, in which prostitutes plied their trade.

whom he recognised as known prostitutes. He watched the girls leave at dawn. In court, for 'keeping a disorderly house' the landlord was fined £1 plus 12s costs.[86] When his licence became due for renewal, it was declined. This led to him being evicted by the pub's owner. One of the prostitutes involved, 17-year-old Susan Lee, later treated the constable concerned to a torrent of verbal abuse, for which she received 7 days' imprisonment.[87]

In 1861, Hastings' police chief Superintendent Glenister called the attention of magistrates to a 'notorious house of ill-fame' in one of the courts of the Bourne. He described frequent disturbances of the peace and felt sure that the owner of the house, Mr. Cox of Halton, knew the character of his tenants. Glenister said that, as at least five prostitutes lived there, it was 'to all intents and purposes a brothel'. Cox told a sergeant that letting the house in this way gained him the most profit, and he intended to continue with it. Glenister said he would appeal to the parish officers of St Clement to do something, and he felt sure that one of the Acts of Parliament would apply to the situation.[88]

Magistrates, too, tried to clean up the town. One in 1861 decided to make an example of Caroline Hennesey, 'a girl of loose character and dashing appearance' by jailing her for seven days with hard labour for the minor offence of being drunk and using obscene language. He stated that there had lately been 'many complaints respecting the disorderly conduct of persons of her class' and declared, ambiguously, that magistrates 'were determined to put a stop to the evil'. Whether he meant the evil of drunk and disorderly conduct, or of prostitution, is unclear.[89]

A number of Hastings' prostitutes cohabited with a man-friend or, more likely, a series of them, for quarrels were often violent and break-ups frequent. Some men lived on their partner's immoral earnings. Other women lived in squalid common lodging-houses and beer-shops, some of which were described by police as 'low brothels' or 'dens of infamy'. Such was the label given to 19 Bourne Street and to a house on the Barrack Ground at Halton which, in its four small rooms, housed ten persons. One of them, Bertha Hewitt, aged 19, was 'a woman of dissipated and wretched appearance' who had dumped her unwanted, illegitimate child in Battle Workhouse. The other occupants were landlady Mrs. Dunk, her son and two daughters, two other suspected prostitutes and three young children.

Many prostitutes were brazen ladies who defended themselves, their associates and their 'patch' passionately and, occasionally, with violence. Some women viewed it simply as a trade. Jane Manser, of 59 All Saints' Street, when charged with being drunk and using obscene language in Robertson Street, said that she wished 'to get an honest living as far as her calling would allow.'[90] If prostitution was a trade then Harriet Clapson was its shop steward. One night Clapson saw Ellen Stanley – 'a showily-dressed woman' - on her 'patch', the *Anchor Inn*, George Street. She marched up to her and accused her of being a rival from London, intent on stealing trade from the locals, and announced 'in language unfit for ears polite' that she did not intend to tolerate her and others plying their vocation in Hastings. Harriet 'proclaimed herself, with a considerable amount of pride, to have been a prostitute in Hastings for ten years and invited Ellen to step outside for a fight, following this up with a violent blow with her fist to Ellen's head. The latter sued and Harriet was fined 10s.[91]

Ann Colvin kept a shop at 11 Albion Street, Halton, above which she ran a brothel. In 1866 she sued (in her husband's name, because of coverture) Caroline Cornelius, a prostitute living with her, for £1. 3s rent and money lent. Caroline told the County Court, 'in a bold manner and in loud tones', that Mrs. Colvin took 'three parts of what she got whilst she was there' – meaning, presumably, that Colvin took three-quarters of her immoral earnings. She also openly admitted in court: 'I get my living by walking the streets'. The Judge found in favour of Colvin and, when Cornelius refused to pay, he said that she would make 'a valuable adjunct' to Lewes prison.[92] The following year, Colvin assaulted an 'unfortunate' attached to another establishment:

> Mrs. Colvin went to complainant's house, and after passing the compliments usual on such occasions, challenged Miss Atkins out to fight. The invitation being declined, Mrs. Colvin pushed complainant and her friend across the room, and 'knocked our heads together', tore complainant's dress, and finished her off by administering a bucket of water shower-bath fashion.[93]

One of the witnesses was Ann Chapman, 'who boldly stated herself to be a prostitute'. Colvin was fined £1 plus costs.

Hastings prostitutes expected the protection of the law. One who was smacked in the face and verbally abused by a man she solicited in Robertson Street went straight to the police. The man, having previous convictions, was sentenced to two months hard labour.

As the population increased, prostitution flourished and by the 1870s about one in every two issues of the local newspaper contained a report mentioning a prostitute. The known clientele belonged to the skilled working class: printers, sailors, plasterers, wheelwrights and boat-builders. This small sample was gleaned from court reports and so includes only those who had complained of being robbed and who did not fear being publicly exposed as users of prostitutes.

REFERENCES

[1] See Wojtczak, H. (2002) *Notable Women of Victorian Hastings*. The Hastings Press.

[2] See Higgs, E. (1989) *Making Sense of the Census*. London.

[3] In comparison, in Paris in 1852, the number of persons employed was 316,000 of whom 112,000 were women; thus, 26% of the Parisian workforce was female. The average wage was 3f 80c (3s 2d) for men and 1f 6c (1s 4½ d) for women.

[4] Parkes, B.R. Statistics as to the Employment of the Female Population of Great Britain. *The Englishwoman's Journal*, 1860.

[5] Her court evidence against a shoplifter.

[6] Brett, T. B. *Historico-Biographies*, Volume I, p.100.

[7] *Hastings & St Leonards Chronicle*, 8 June 1864.

[8] During some research I assumed that the first woman stationmaster, in 1832, performed only 'ladylike' functions, given women's restrictive clothing. However, I later discovered that a railway historian had witnessed her climbing tall signal-ladders to light paraffin lamps. Wojtczak, H. (2002) *Women Workers on the Railways*. The Hastings Press.

[9] Brett owned a newspaper, kept chronicles and wrote reminiscences.

[10] Longfield later became St Mary's Terrace, Plynlimmon Road and Priory Road.

[11] Brett, T. B. *Histories,* Volume 1 and 1851 Census.

[12] Brett, T. B. *Histories,* Volume 2.

[13] Brett, T. B. *Histories* Volume 5. p37

[14] *Hastings & St Leonards News,* 8 May 1863.

[15] *The Fisherman's Home* no longer exists.

[16] The *Merry Christmas* no longer exists.

[17] Report to the General Board of Health, 1850.

[18] In the 1840s they moved to the *Swan Shades.*

[19] Located at what is now the east end of Marine Court.

[20] Brett, T. B. *Histories,* Volume 1.

[21] It later became the Dispensary.

[22] Argos now occupies the site.

[23] At the *Hare & Hounds* they staged plays and musical events.

[24] By the Town Clerk, J. G. Shorter.

[25] *Hastings & St Leonards Herald & Observer,* 9 September 1872.

[26] He applied for protection and she was bound over in sureties of £25 to be of good behaviour for six months. *Hastings & St Leonards Independent,* 4 December 1874.

[27] Since demolished and replaced with a supermarket. A discount store occupies the site.

[28] She died in 1869, aged 48.

[29] It is now a private residence.

[30] 1793 Court Sessions Book.

[31] *Hastings & St Leonards News,* 23 July 1862

[32] *Hastings Independent and East Sussex News,* 26 June 1874

[33] *Hastings & St Leonards Observer,* 27 August 1867.

[34] Manwaring Baines, J., list of licensees, Hastings Museum collection.

[35] Pinchbeck, I. (1930) *Women Workers and the Industrial Revolution.* Virago reprint 1981, p295

[36] Step-daughter of J. S. Mill.

[37] In 1862, one of them, Charles Blake, committed suicide on the premises by shooting himself behind the counter.

[38] Brett, T. B. *Historico-Biographies,* Volume 2, p.167

[39] On the site of present-day Tower Road.

[40] Brett, T. B. *Histories,* Volume 1.

[41] Now Queen's Road.

[42] Her son, to give him his due, saved at least five people from drowning during his long career on the machines.

[43] *Hastings & St Leonards News,* 8 September 1865.

[44] Manwaring Baines, J. (1955) *Historic Hastings.* Parsons, Hastings. p305

[45] They later opened a lodging house at 43 Marina.

[46] They also let houses.

[47] See Wojtczak, H.(2002) *Notable Women of Victorian Hastings.* The Hastings Press.

[48] The 'fly' was introduced in Brighton in 1816.

[49] Manwaring Baines, J., unpublished list of trades, Hastings Museum collection.

[50] From 'Milaner' a man from Milan who imported and sold small articles of a miscellaneous kind.

[51] A fur shoulder cape with hanging ends; often consisting of the fur of a fox.

[52] The clock was, and still is, on the Old Town Hall building, now a Museum.

[53] Beer.

[54] *Hastings & St Leonards News,* 20 April 1860

[55] *Hastings & St Leonards News,* 12 October 1860

[56] *Hastings & St Leonards News,* 12 October 1860

[57] *Hastings & St Leonards News,* 19 October, 1860

[58] See Wojtczak, H. (2002) *Notable Women of Victorian Hastings.* The Hastings Press.

[59] NADFAS Church Recording Group (1983) *St. Mary Magdalen Church 1852-1982* In 1866, a new organ was built by Holdich.

[60] Brett. T. B. *Historico-biographies,* Volume 6 p.60.

[61] Now Russell St.

[62] *Hastings & St Leonards Observer,* 13 February 1937.

[63] This was rebuilt in 1896 and is now an office of Hastings Borough Council.

[64] The boys' school was opened under the Baptist Church at Wellington Square.

[65] This had no playground, so children assembled in the street.

[66] Possibly the same Mrs. Tebay previously at St Clement's Place School.

[67] Pinchbeck, I. (1930) *Women Workers and the Industrial Revolution.* Virago reprint 1981, p285.

[68] All Saints' Poorhouse was in Old London Road and that of St Leonards was a thatched cottage in Tivoli.

[69] Manwaring Baines, J. (1955) *Historic Hastings.* Parsons, Hastings. p136-9

[70] The gaol was used only as a lock-up after 1856, prisoners were held instead at Lewes Gaol.

[71] In London a Lady Superintendent had sole charge of the Female Prison and 600 inmates, assisted by a deputy and forty matrons. Parkes, B.R. (1859) *What Can Educated Women Do?*

[72] The Bonds' residence was 4 George Street, which later became the Post Office under a different Postmaster. Manwaring Baines, J. (1955) *Historic Hastings.* Parsons, Hastings. p297-8

[73] Peak, S. (1985) *Fishermen of Hastings.* p.30

[74] Peak, S. (1985) *Fishermen of Hastings.* pp. 30-31

[75] *Hastings & St Leonards News*, 15 August 1864.

[76] See Wojtczak, H. (2002) *Notable Women of Victorian Hastings.* The Hastings Press.

[77] *Hastings & St Leonards News*, 27 June 1862.

[78] Boucherett, J. (1862) *On the Choice of a Business.*

[79] Held in Hastings Reference Library.

[80] *Hastings & St Leonards News*, 22 February 1856

[81] *Hastings & St Leonards Observer*, 13 February 1937, and reminiscences from T. B. Brett, 1896.

[82] *London Labour and the London Poor,* Volume 1, 1861

[83] Patmore, C. *Unthrift.* (date unknown).

[84] *Hastings & St Leonards News,* 19 January 1856.

[85] *Hastings & St Leonards News*, 26 Jan 1855.

[86] In 1863 the previous landlord's disabled daughter had been raped on the premises.

[87] *Hastings & St Leonards News*, 19 August 1864.

[88] *Hastings & St Leonards News*,17 May 1861.

[89] *Hastings & St Leonards News*, 15 February 1861.

[90] *Hastings & St Leonards Chronicle*, 14 August 1872.

[91] *Hastings & St Leonards Herald & Observer*, 24 June 1871

[92] *Hastings & St Leonards News*, 14 July 1865.

[93] *Hastings & St Leonards News*, 23 February 1866.

Home Life & Leisure

LUXURY & POVERTY

The rich man in his castle;
the poor man at his gate
God made them, high and lowly;
and ordered their estate.[1]

There was in the mid-19th century greater discrepancy between the living standards of the middle class and those of the working class than is the case today. Then, it was usual for every middle-class household to employ two or three domestic servants, and they had the space to house them, too. Concurrently, thousands of Hastingers lived on, and sometimes below, the breadline, in conditions of appalling overcrowding.

Homes of the rich

The well-off began to come to Hastings in the late 18th century and when James Burton founded St Leonards in the late 1820s it, too, became a fashionable watering place for the wealthy, who came for reasons of health or recreation. Some settled permanently but more came for a month, a season, or an open-ended sojourn. There were few titled ladies among the permanent residents, but gentry appeared in almost every list of visitors published weekly by the local press. Visitors might stay with friends, lease a house or apartments, or rent rooms in boarding- or lodging-houses - the most expensive were those along the Marina, Grand Parade and Eversfield Place. Boarding-houses were a little like hotels. In 1824, Moss remarked that 'an individual is enabled, for the moderate sum of £2.12s 6d per week ... to live in the most sumptuous manner'.[2] Wealthy visitors generally brought with them their upper servants - such as a lady's maid and a governess if there were children – while lower servants were engaged locally, generally by the proprietor of the establishment.

Those of the wealthy who were permanently resident lived mainly in St Leonards, although some parts of Hastings 'new town' were favoured, such as Wellington Square, Pelham Place, Pelham Crescent and Caroline Place. In the Old Town, Old London Road contained a few substantial houses, inhabited by the MP, magistrates and other prominent persons. By 1850, the majority of the well-off were abandoning the Old Town for the more salubrious and modern St Leonards, where many houses were built with the very latest in luxurious fittings – i.e., piped water and flush WCs.

The wealthy lived in spacious opulence: it was common for just two or three persons to occupy a house with three or four large reception-rooms, several bedrooms, servant's quarters, stabling and extensive gardens, and for servants to outnumber the family. At The Mansion, opposite All Saints' Church, the Earl and Countess of Waldegrave and the Earl's two daughters were looked after by 12 live-in servants: a housekeeper, two lady's maids, two housemaids, a kitchen-maid, butler, coachman, footman, groom, house-lad and stable boy. Lady Boothby,[3] a former comedy actress, lived at Rosemount, St Leonards, a 17-room villa with very large drawing and dining rooms, gardens, stabling and a private theatre in which she gave performances for selected guests.

Among St Leonards' aristocratic visitors were Princess Sophia Of Gloucester and Edinburgh (1773-1844) who, after three months at Bohemia House, moved to (what is now called) Gloucester Lodge, Maze Hill, in 1831. Princess Victoria (1819-1901) spent the winter of 1834 at 57 Marina and her aunt, the King's widow, Dowager Queen Adelaide (1792-1849), stayed at Seymour Place (now known as Adelaide House, Grand Parade) in 1837.[4] Throughout the century the town continued to be blessed with the patronage of the gentry and nobility including many foreign royals, such as Queen Christiana of Spain, who leased 88-89 Marina in 1862, and Empress Eugenie, a French refugee who stayed at the Marine Hotel in 1870. Many other aristocratic, eminent, famous or notable women visited or lived in Hastings around the mid-century.[5]

Although wealthy ladies did not need to earn a living, they were far from 'unoccupied'. Their days were filled with overseeing servants, choosing menus, checking household accounts, seeing dressmakers, shopping, taking carriage-rides, correspondence, reading, sketching, playing music, singing, embroidery and needlework as well as doing the round of social visits to other ladies of their class. Ladies were expected to change costumes frequently, at the very least from day-dresses to evening gowns. In the evenings there were talks and lectures, concerts, quadrille parties and soirées dansantes. The *Brighton Guardian* described St Leonards in 1847 as:

> the gayest of the gay. Balls, dinner-parties, fancy-fairs, pic-nics, archery-meetings, riding-parties, cricket-matches, shooting-competitions, boating-excursions ... Among the balls and card- assemblies in the Old Town are one at the Swan, one at the King's Head and two at the Royal Oak, all well-attended'.[6]

Mrs. Fletcher Norton, Hastings' most celebrated hostess of the 1850s, held many dances and dinner parties at her large, elegant house at 4 Wellington Square. There was always a live orchestra and the hand-picked guests included the most prominent persons in town. At one party 'the large drawing room and the ballroom adjoining were filled with beauty and fashionables'. The one hundred affluent guests included the MP Frederick North, his daughter Marianne[7] and a smattering of aristocrats and knights. Several grand country houses were the venues for bachelor's dances and huge fancy dress balls were held at Beauport by Thomas Brassey, MP and his wife Anna.[8] Their guest list included every top society 'name' in Sussex. Pheasant, partridge and exotic fruits from hot-houses were laid out during a break in the dancing. The newspaper reports of tables 'groaning' with the weight of all the delicacies of the season stand in stark contrast to the adjacent reports about hundreds of starving workers being doled a controlled portion of dry bread and watery soup in Hastings' charity-kitchens.

Homes of the poor

Although many wives worked, they still performed the daily household chores, and without any labour-saving devices. Fetching water from a well, emptying chamber-pots and beating rugs were everyday chores in a working class household. Few of the poor even had ovens and they had to subsist on open-fire pan cooking, or take their meat to a bakery to be cooked. Luckily in Hastings there was always a good supply of fresh fish and seafood, because until the 1870s the Victorian working class diet was unhealthy. A lot of cheap food was adulterated, and hygiene was not thought to be an issue.

Among the poor there was terrible overcrowding in the 1850s. In the grid bounded by Market Passage and Alfred Street, St Leonards, cottages of five small rooms, kitchen and scullery typically housed ten to 14 persons. Tenants would sub-let part of their homes; in one case a couple and their six sons aged from 18 to five lived in two rooms. Market Passage was home to 84 residents in just 16 small tenements. Hastings Old Town was worse, and was appallingly unsanitary. The narrow, gas-lit alleyways and steep paths were crammed with tiny, badly constructed homes.[9] Much of the accommodation was over two hundred years old and had no drainage, running water or flush toilets. The Bourne stream was like an open sewer and the stench in summer was nauseating. Privies (earth closets) were shared between many families and they overflowed into yards and, sometimes, even into houses. Homes were gloomy and there was widespread dampness. Most houses were under-ventilated, lit with oil lamps and heated with coal fires, and they were dangerous to live in: many people were burnt or even killed when paraffin lamps exploded or dresses caught fire.

Life in a railway hut

The most important event in mid-Victorian Hastings & St Leonards was the extension of the railway line to the area, which necessitated massive earthworks to create four tunnels. But the towns could not house the 3,000 railway labourers, known as navvies, who began to arrive from 1849. Once all the lodgings had been taken, a large number of families were obliged to scrabble a miserable existence in makeshift shanties with addresses such as 'Hut at top of Mount Pleasant Tunnel'. In these huts, women struggled to bring up, typically, three or four children, devoid of any household conveniences or basic utilities, such as water or drainage. Amazingly, one couple with six children under 12 even had a lodger.

The well-to do ladies of St Leonards were shocked and horrified to witness on their very doorstep people who (in their genteel eyes) were 'sunk in the most deplorable state of degradation and sin'. Their distress led to 'rescue work', which amounted to the collection and distribution of alms, and a school being provided for the children.

The men worked hard, drank hard, and fought hard. They caused one hell of a rumpus in town with their drunken, riotous brawling and fist-fights in the streets. Their conduct towards their wives when they staggered back, drunk, to the dismal, cold residence full of whining, hungry children can only be imagined. Records show that some wives and children of navvies ended up in the Hastings Union Workhouse at Cackle Street.

Safety precautions were extremely lax at the railway works and hundreds of men were injured - some very seriously - in rock falls, tunnel collapses and by runaway wagons. After emergency medical treatment they were cared for by their wives during months of convalescence. The works created a number of widows: fourteen fatalities were recorded. Sometimes a son took his late father's job at the works. One, an 11 year old, supported his widowed mother and two siblings aged seven and four. Another, a boy of ten, was run over and killed by some wagons as he oiled them.

OUT & ABOUT

The Seaside

Hastings' major attraction was, of course, the sea, which was believed to have health-giving properties and which was used both for drinking and immersion. Much fuss was also made (by the owners) of the healthful properties of the drinking water from the Chalybeate springs in West Hill Road and St Andrews Gardens. Sea water was supplied at 3d a bucket to lodging-houses and even piped into some residences. Bathing was governed by strict regulations: the 30 bathing machines were allocated by gender, women's machines were kept 75 yards away from those of men and boats were not allowed to come within 50 yards. Customers were 'dipped' by bathing attendants of their own sex. No-one was allowed to bathe in the open sea from 'Rock-a-Noir'[10] to St Leonards until 1855, when men only were permitted to do so. There were several indoor bathing establishments and, in 1864, Turkish Baths were opened at 2 West Hill Road, St Leonards. The owners charged ladies double the fee men paid to use identical facilities. In keeping with the morality of the day, the sexes were kept apart most effectively by restricting women to two days a week.[11]

On the beach, donkeys were hired for rides and shabby hawkers sold small items and refreshments, while 'gypsies' offered to tell fortunes. Boat trips were available to Eastbourne, Brighton, London and Boulogne. Yachts and rowing boats could be hired below the Parade and yachting regattas had been held since 1820. In 1843, when Queen Victoria and Prince Albert steamed past Hastings on their way from Brighton, hundreds of people lined the Parade, dressed in all their finery. Any man entitled to a uniform wore it. Banners were waved, royal salutes fired and the Union Flag hoisted at many places. It was reported that 'Every eye was strained towards the noble vessel', but whether the royal couple noticed the loyal accolades and festivities is unrecorded.

A ladies' bathing machine in the 1850s.

In and out of town

Jaunts around town on foot, horseback or carriage were popular, to take in Hastings' restorative and curative air while seeing the sights and hearing the sounds. The sights included the Russian Gun, a symbolic tribute to Crimean casualties, placed near Pelham Crescent in 1857, the Albert Memorial (1863) and the Waldegrave Drinking Fountain (1861). The sounds included an excess of music. The Town Band had been established in 1822 and from 1852 it played three times a week in Warrior Square Gardens. There were multifarious street-musicians, singers, buskers, organ-grinders, banjo-strummers and hurdy-gurdy players. Before long visitors and residents began to complain about the incessant noise.

One major pastime for women was browsing the fashionable shops at the Colonnade, Castle Street and Wellington Place as well as the alcove stalls in Pelham Arcade, which had opened in 1825. In 1859 a second Arcade of ten shops was opened, linking Cambridge Road with Havelock Road. From the 1860s Robertson Street was the smartest place to shop, and was known as the 'Regent Street' of Hastings.

The biggest tourist attractions were Hastings Castle and St Clements' Caves, both of which were opened to the public in the 1820s. Horse racing took place at Bulverhythe from 1828 until 1865. Carriage-drives were popular, to see outlying villages and beauty spots including Ecclesbourne Glen, Ore, Hollington, Bodiam, Northiam, Old Roar, Camber Castle, Dripping Well, Battle, Icklesham and Brede. After 1846 railway excursions were available and in 1851 many Hastingers attended the Great Exhibition in London.

The Church

English society was still intensely religious at this date and services and other church-related activities were extremely well-attended, particularly by middle-class women. The four main churches - All Saints', St Clement's, St Mary's and St Leonards – were already overcrowded by 1850 and the population was still on the increase. It was a frequent complaint that men could hardly get inside a church, female patronage being so overwhelming, and women spilled over onto the men's side of segregated pews.

To counteract this overcrowding, in the 1850s and 60s a number of new churches were built, towards which women gave considerable financial support. But as soon as the first - St Mary Magdalen Church - opened in 1852 the seating was already insufficient. The incumbent purchased at his own expense several benches, each seating 70, which were 'filled to utmost'. Another new church was desperately needed and it was a woman - Lady St John – who bore the entire cost of building Christ Church, in 'a part of St Leonards containing the mass of the poor, 3,000 in number'. Lady St John laid the foundation stone in 1859 and her son was the first incumbent. Within ten years this church also proved to be too small and a larger edifice was built next door in 1873. Within one year this, too, was suffering from such severe overcrowding that 'a Visitor' complained in the local press that she was so cramped in the ladies' pews that 'the movement of either hand or foot became ... well-nigh an impossibility'.[12]

The power of the Christian religion in mid-19th-century England should not be underestimated. The working classes were told by their social superiors that their lowly position in life was His Will and part of His Great Scheme. Many of the poor rejected religion, but to be considered 'respectable' - and thereby obtain financial assistance - even the destitute had to embrace religion, or pretend to. Advertisements for servants' positions often specified that applicants must be church-goers, and servants' attendance at Sunday services was often compulsory.

Archery

The fashionable sport for genteel ladies was archery. Queen Victoria herself gave 20 guineas a year for the purchase of a gold bracelet[13] to be presented to the lady St Leonards Archer gaining the most points during the season. The lady archers had a uniform consisting of a white dress with a green silk scarf fastened at the left shoulder by a special badge, which was in the shape of a silver-gilt shield bearing an arrow, with *Victoria* embossed on a raised scroll, and the society's monogram surmounted by a crown. A white straw hat trimmed with green velvet and white ostrich feathers completed the outfit. The uniform was abandoned in 1863, the badge only being retained. Archery meetings were held from the Queen's birthday, May 24th, until October and were very popular: one at St Leonards in 1865 attracted 73 contestants and over 500 spectators. Scores, prizes and attendees were reported in the local press, and a brass band played throughout, always finishing with the National Anthem. In the evening, a Grand Archery Ball was often held. Anna Kingsford[14] attended some archery meetings in St Leonards with her mother in the 1860s as did the famous actress Fanny Kemble, on her occasional visits. The exiled French Royal Family also attended during their stay in the 1860s.

Public houses

Working class women often went to pubs to escape the wretched surroundings in which they lived, but the respectable were accompanied by their husbands, who would usually take them to a slightly better class of pub than their 'usual', or into the saloon instead of the public bar. Pubs ranged in size from small rooms accommodating ten to 15 standing people to large taverns offering accommodation; they ranged in style from dingy beer shops with bare wooden benches, filled with sweaty, carousing fishermen to spacious establishments with etched glass windows, velvet seating, French-polished rosewood bars, gleaming brass fittings and immense lamps hanging from lofty ceilings.

Above: Shepherd Street, St Leonards. These early-19th century cottages, comprising just 6 small rooms, typically housed eight to fifteen persons by the mid century.

Below: The Bottle, cold, misery and want destroy their child An impoverished home where an infant has just died.. Etching by George Cruikshank..

The sale of drink was considerable and the pubs numerous; indeed trade was so brisk that landlords regularly broke the law by serving out-of-hours. In working-class pubs activities included buying and eating seafood and chestnuts from hawkers; singing, especially ballads, gambling -though this was strictly against the license - and telling yarns. On many a night the Old Town saw drunken revellers singing and fighting in its streets. Many windows were broken, as were more than a few heads.

Educational recreation

With no television, cinema or radio, audio-visual information was transmitted via lectures, talks and lantern slide-shows. The Literary & Scientific Institution, founded in 1831, offered a reduced subscription for women: they paid 15s, the same as minors, instead of the £2 paid by men. Two ladies were among the honorary members, and one, Countess Waldegrave, was a life member. The society forbade lectures on politics, and this meant that women's rights could not be discussed.

At the Mechanic's Institution many women attended presentations, illustrated with lantern-slides, on subjects such as the Holy lands, astronomy and the evils of alcoholic liquor or slavery. At one lecture President Alfred Burton expressed pleasure at the large number of ladies present, and remarked with relief that he had no fear of Bloomerism (i.e. feminism) amongst them.

Evening schools run by the churches were generally reserved for male youths but one opened for fisher-folk, held during the winter in the Fishermen's Clubroom, admitted all persons aged 21 and over. Mondays and Wednesdays were reserved for women and girls over 14. A Ladies' Educational Association was founded in the early 1870s.

The Philosophical Society was established in 1858 and accepted female members, although it reported in 1859 that none of 'the fair sex' had yet joined. The founders forbade women to address the audience; indeed, as late as 1882 physician Dr. Anna Kingsford was forbidden to read out her paper on anti-vivisection. Luckily, other venues welcomed lady lecturers, readers and performers. Mrs. Balfour spoke on Self-Education in 1850 and, at the Mechanics' Institution, Miss Balfour gave a talk on Charlotte Brontë in 1860. At the Ragged School, Mrs. Wightman lectured on total abstinence in 1864. The largest crowd ever assembled in Hastings to hear one woman speak was the estimated 2,500 who crowded into a circus tent on Priory Meadows in 1874 to hear Catherine Mumford Booth preach the gospel. She was an evangelist, a co-founder (with her husband) of the Salvation Army, and the century's most passionate advocate of female preachers.

Men, women, children, - from the fisher-boy and flower girl up to members of the School Board and Town Council, publicans and Good Templars, young sparks whose god is a cigar and a fresh-looking cravat, milliner-girls radiant in ribbons and cheap finery, shop-boys, tradesmen

Caution to Young Ladies who ride in Crinoline
on Donkeys

saints and sinners - all were gathered…Who was this woman who possesses such power as to attract to a single meeting at least one-tenth of our borough? Was it to hear a woman preach - because some of us believe that ladies have no right to be our theological teachers - that we went?[15]

Although it is likely that the huge crowd attended mainly to gawp at a woman preacher as though she were a circus sideshow, Booth saw her vocation from a feminist perspective:

There seems to be a great deal of unnecessary fear of women occupying any position which involves publicity, lest she should be rendered unfeminine by the indulgence of ambition or vanity; but why should woman any more than man be charged with ambition when impelled to use her talents for the good of her race.[16]

Entertainment

Many female entertainers came to Hastings, as circus acts, singers, actresses and musicians. A travelling menagerie, owned by Mrs. Wombwell, and the American Female Serenaders were among the popular shows. Fanny Kemble[17] gave readings from Shakespeare to huge audiences at the *Swan,* at George Street Hall, and at the St Leonards Assembly Rooms. In 1856 Miss P. Horton, a gifted impressionist, performed in Hastings, caricaturing everyone 'from servant girl to Savoyard musician'.

The subscription fees of libraries, reading rooms, societies and gardens, and the ticket prices for theatre performances placed many out of the reach of working people. Cheaper, low-brow entertainment included Ginette's French Circus, which visited in 1853 and 1864. Its attractions, which included ceiling-walking, ensured that Priory Meadows was crowded to overflowing. At the Rock Fair, held annually in the vicinity of Cuckoo Hill, lots of women and men got drunk, gambled and engaged in brawls. Thieves found it the ideal place to pick pockets. Described as a 'grievous moral pest' it was ceased by order of the authorities in 1861.

Informal dances, fêtes and carnivals were held and Ann Page (née Noakes), known as 'Old Nanny', whose date of birth is given variously as 1766 or 1788, was said to attend them all. She was the widow of a revenue officer who had died in 1825. The day after Queen Victoria's coronation in 1838 Mrs. Page, 'a sprightly widow of 72' (or 50), was 'crowned' Queen of All Saints in a frolicsome ceremony at which prominent local dignitaries, including Frederick North MP, joined in the fun by playing Lords-in-Waiting. Mr C. J. Jeudwine,[18] as the Archbishop of Canterbury, crowned Old Nanny on a platform erected across the road on the high pavement between 39 and 117 High Street. Shortly afterwards Nanny was drenched with water and her dress was ruined. She lived in All Saints' Street and was buried in All Saints' Church yard.

Mid-Victorian women squeezed into pews in overcrowded churches.

Charity Work

> I have often heard it regretted that ladies have no stated employment, no profession. It is a mistake: charity is the calling of a lady; the care of the poor is her profession ... Women of fortune have abundant leisure which can no way be so properly or pleasantly filled up.
>
> Hannah More, 1809

Hastings and, especially, St Leonards attracted a large number of single ladies and widows of private means. The 1851 Census showed that women comprised 79% of those enumerated as 'Persons of Rank or property', and 11.6% of females (compared with just 5.8% of males) enjoyed an unearned income derived from investments in business, annuities, pensions, allowances given by relations, giving mortgages, and letting ground or buildings; one gave her occupation as 'Proprietor of Coffee Estates in Ceylon'. Ninety-two women were house or land proprietors in 1851 and, in 1861, three-quarters of those who derived income from property rental were women. In addition, there were many women who were supported by wealthy fathers and husbands. Such women could not seek paid work, partly because it would bring shame upon the family, but also because the professions were closed to them, and humbler jobs were beneath them.

In the 19th century the only welfare assistance given by statutory means was through a poor-rate, which supported the workhouses and gave a (very) few persons an allowance known as 'parish relief'. All other

redistribution of wealth was voluntary. The collection and dispersal of charitable donations became the occupation of spinsters, widows and wives of rich men, who had plenty of time and resources and a desire to 'do something' for society and to be engaged in a fulfilling occupation. The management of the poor was a thoroughly acceptable public channel for women's energy and ingenuity and the only way for their organisational and financial skills to receive public recognition. Only in charity work could ladies play an active and prominent role in public life, hold offices such as organiser, treasurer and secretary and have their names and addresses listed in directories and other documents.

With energy and determination ladies founded, organised and managed a large number of institutions and societies. Working for charitable organisations afforded ladies a great deal of social kudos and gave them the opportunity to rub shoulders with local dignitaries such as the Countess Waldegrave, her neighbour Miss Kingsbury, the Sayer heiresses, and Arabella North, sister of the local MP. For some, it amounted to a career. One, Charlotte Menella Lutwidge of 2 Wellington Square, spent her whole life devoted to charity work in Hastings. Her death in 1857 was said to be 'deeply regretted by both the pick and the poor'.

In 1839 charity-ladies held a three-day bazaar in the Pelham Arcade in aid of an Infirmary. They had secured the patronage of Queen Adelaide and the stalls were manned by girls of the best families, including the MP's daughter, Marianne North. They raised £538. When the Ragged School in the Old Town became overcrowded, and £500 was needed to build new premises, a group of ladies raised £390 in just three days by holding a bazaar, at which 175 well-heeled customers spent an average of 5s each – half a week's wages for a labouring woman. Among the ladies' other successes were a Home for Invalid Gentlewomen, opened in 1855, and a Young Women's Christian Association, opened in Norman Road East in 1866, with bible classes given by the Countess of Aberdeen.

Ladies were also involved in Temperance Societies, prompted by the desire to relieve the suffering of wives and children at the hands of drunken men. One, the St Mary Magdalen Improvement & Recreation Society, was based at Alfred Street. Here, ladies were keen to show the working man that fun could be had without alcohol. Occasionally, they provided the amusements themselves. In 1861 at St Mary Magdalen National School, a musical treat was presented to 350 of the working class by a concert-party of a dozen ladies and gentlemen. When the performance was repeated for a middle-class audience, it was held at a more prestigious venue - the St Leonards Assembly rooms. There was gender division even in charity work. Causes connected with maternity, children, religion, health and education were seen as the province of ladies; but when fishermen were lost at sea it was gentlemen who launched Relief Funds for the widows and children. However, they still left the donkey work such as the day-to-day fundraising, and the door-to-door collecting, to the ladies.

The philanthropic work carried out by ladies to help the destitute poor is included in *Down & Out in Victorian Hastings* (forthcoming) and is not, therefore, repeated here.

MUSIC HALL, HASTINGS.

FOR TWO NIGHTS ONLY.

MONDAY & TUESDAY, AUGUST 16 & 17.

THE Eminent LONDON STAR of COMEDY and SONG,

MISS EMMA STANLEY,

The Great Artiste, Pianist, Harpist, Guitarist, Vocalist, and Delineator, in her Celebrated Entertainment THE SEVEN AGES OF WOMAN! written expressly for her by E. L. BLANCHARD, Esq., in which she will personate Thirty-six entirely Original and Distinct Characters, with performances on the Pianoforte, Harp, Guitar, and German Zether: and Songs in French, Italian, German, Dutch and English.

MUSIC HALL, HASTINGS.

One Representation only, TUESDAY, AUGUST the 23rd, 1864.

Grand Ethiopian Entertainment by the celebrated

FEMALE CHRISTY'S MINSTRELS,

AS given before His Royal Highness the Prince of Wales, consisting of Songs, Duets, Glees, Dances, Jokes, &c., peculiar to the Indian and Negro Race.

Stalls (numbered and reserved), 3s.; unreserved seats, 2s.; back seats, 1s.; promenade, 6d. Tickets to be obtained at Mr. Lockey's Pianoforte Warehouse, under the Music Hall.

Doors open at 7.30 p.m. To commence at 8. Entrance to the promenade in Havelock road.

ANOTHER COMPLAINT.

SIR,—I am extremely fond of music, and on week-days listen with pleasure to the excellent strains of the German Band which plays in Wellington square. But on every Sunday afternoon, for nearly three hours, the square rings again with what I at first thought was a stentorian band of screech-owls, hyænas, and peacocks, accompanied by a harpsichord of railway-locomotive power and energy. This pandemonial music affects, I presume, to be sacred; but the yells and screams entirely drown all the character of musical composition.

Pray, sir, ask this squadron of young ladies to spare the ears and permit the Sabbatic reflections of

A NEIGHBOUR.

Wellington square, June 14, 1868.

Politics

Among the reasons for denying women the parliamentary vote was that they took no interest in politics; another was that political campaigns were too rough for women, being delicate and sensitive. In reality, in Hastings as everywhere women attended the hustings and some took as much or more interest as men, both by way of partisanship and by rowdiness. At the riotous 1852 election fishwives jostled and punched the candidates as they visited the Old Town. Jane Smith, a baker of 56 High Street, was accused of supplying flour for hooligans to hurl at candidates - a slander she strongly denied in a letter to the local paper. She had innocently sold bread to a woman, unaware of its intended use as a missile to be directed at candidates.

Although women were excluded from local government, in 1861 a group of ladies sent a memorial (petition) to the Borough Council protesting against a proposed commercial harbour. The main part of it read:

> The opinions, feelings and wishes of the Ladies of Hastings and St Leonards on this question having been unrepresented, the Persons whose names and residences are appended being owners of property or the wives of owners of Property, residents and unmarried Ladies residing with their families, visitors, Lodging house keepers, wives of Tradesmen and Householders interested in the trade and prosperity of the place, wish to record their formal protest against the adoption of the proposed scheme.
>
> The Memorialists ... feel imperatively called upon the express their conviction that a Port and Packet Station are not only unnecessary and uncalled for but would be highly detrimental to the moral and social condition as well as the material interests of these towns. Their establishment will altogether alter and deteriorate the character of the place, depreciate the Value of first class House property and injure the present trade by keeping away the better class of Residents and Visitors as has been proved in the case of Southampton and Weymouth and other places; and that the Privacy and Liberty so greatly prized by the female portion and which have been hitherto among the chief recommendations of the place, will be entirely destroyed.
>
> But the all-important consideration that the Memorialists have most at heart, and without which they would not have ventured to put themselves forward on the present occasions is the well-known fact of the tendency of the Sea Port and Packet Stations to demoralize the neighbouring Population in various ways and by the increase of Sunday trains, Sunday work and Sunday trading to aggravate and extend the desecration of the Sabbath.
>
> In certain localities Sea Ports and Packet Stations with their objectionable but unavoidable accompaniments are a necessary evil which must be borne with and counterracted as best it may, but to introduce the evil gratuitously and without necessity instead of being thankful for the exemption, is to cast away a precious privilege and to deal a heavy blow to the religious, moral and social interests of these towns.

The first signatories were the Countess of Waldegrave and her step daughter Elizabeth, and the vast majority of the rest gave addresses in Grand Parade, Eversfield Place and Warrior Square.[19] The harbour was never built.

Above Electioneering at the hustings, 1865. One of the arguments against giving in women the vote was that they were not interested in politics. This photograph shows many local women among the crowds on Priory Meadow.
Photograph reproduced courtesy of Hastings Museum and Art Gallery

Below Pelham Arcade in the 1830s. A very popular shopping place, in which women ran small retail businesses: a female stall-holder can just be seen on the far right. The arcade is now disused, but its elegant iron roof struts can still be seen in the foyer café of St Mary in the Castle Arts Centre.

REFERENCES

The heading quote is from Hannah More is from *Coelebs in Search of a Wife*.

[1] Alexander, Mrs. C. *All Things Bright and Beautiful*. The verse is omitted from modern versions.

[2] Moss, W.G. (1824) *The History and Antiquities of the Town and Port Hastings*. p.168-9

[3] See Wojtczak, H. (2002) *Notable Women of Victorian Hastings*. The Hastings Press.

[4] Ibid.

[5] Short biographies of Barbara Bodichon, Sophia Jex Blake, Marianne North and Bessie Rayner Parkes appear in Wojtczak, H.(2002) *Notable Women of Victorian Hastings*..

[6] Quoted in Brett, T. B. *Histories* Volume 3.

[7] See Volume 2.

[8] See Volume 2.

[9] Much of this area was destroyed between 1928-1963 when the council demolished hundreds of buildings. A busy main road, The Bourne, was built right through the middle.

[10] Now Rock-a-Nore.

[11] The Turkish bath company went bankrupt in 1869.

[12] *Hastings & St Leonards Chronicle*, 22 May 1874.

[13] The 1839 bracelet is held at the Victoria & Albert Museum.

[14] See Volume 2.

[15] *Hastings & St Leonards News* 13 July 1874.

[16] Booth, C. M., (1859) *Female Ministry; or, Woman's Right to Preach the Gospel*.

[17] Fanny Kemble, 1809-1893. Famous Shakespearean actress and divorcee. She attracted many distinguished men including George Stephenson, who invited her to the opening of the Liverpool and Manchester Railway.

[18] Grocer and cheese-monger of 117 High St.

[19] The Memorial is held in Hastings Museum.

INDECENT EXPOSURE.—*Mary Ann Barnes* (known as "Portsmouth Poll"), a prostitute, was charged with indecent exposure of her person.

Police-constable Henry Dennis proved having found the prisoner committing the act described in the charge, on Saturday night about eleven o'clock, in the road at the back of the Infirmary.

Defendant attributed her bad conduct to having had some intoxicating liquor given her. From the statements made, it appeared prisoner's conduct was of a most shameless character.

It being her first appearance, she escaped with ten days' imprisonment only, instead of the full term named in the Vagrancy Act.

MONDAY, OCTOBER 11.—Before T. Ross, Esq.

DRUNKEN CHARGES.—*Ann Miles*, an elderly woman, whose face betokened a love of strong drink, was charged with being drunk and using bad language.

Police-constable Wilson found prisoner in London road, St. Mary Magdalen, on Saturday night, at a quarter-past ten, very drunk, holding a lamp-post, and swearing at a mob of boys who had assembled. She would not go away, and was locked up.

Prisoner said a "drop of drink" which she had had given her had "overcome" her. She was very sorry.

CROSS-SUMMONSES BY LADIES.—*Mrs Mary Smith* summoned *Mrs. Harriet Leper* and *Mrs. Susan Taylor* for an assault, and they in their turn summoned *Mrs. Smith* for a similar infringement of the laws. Mr. Davenport-Jones represented Mrs. Leper and Mrs. Taylor. The parties, to use the words of the advocate, are all "fish women," and Mrs. Leper and Mrs. Taylor are sisters; they are also partners in business, the one carrying the tray and the other pushing the barrow. There seems to have been a jealously in connection with professional affairs existing between them for some time, and matters came to a climax, when they met at White Rock, on Saturday the 29th ult. Sundry civilities were exchanged and sundry bows, and then there was a race for the office of the Magistrates' Clerk for the "taking out" of summonses. — The Bench fined Mrs Smith 10s. and costs £1. The others were dismissed.

Women & the Law

Crimes of Women

Mid-Victorian Hastings women committed a wide range of misdemeanours including assault, drink-related offences, using obscene language, sleeping out, being an idle person, wilful damage, receiving stolen goods and murder. Crimes resulting directly from poverty are dealt will be dealt with in *Down & Out in Victorian Hastings* (forthcoming) and will not be included here.

In the 1860s about one in five persons arrested was female but this rose to one in four of those charged with assault. For simple larceny the sexes were convicted in roughly equal numbers. A quarter of persons summonsed for being drunk were female but nearly two-thirds of women were discharged compared with only one-third of men. For all other offences, 40% of women were acquitted compared with just 26% of men.[1] This may indicate that the police were overzealously arresting women without good cause, or that magistrates were more lenient towards the 'fairer sex' than towards their own.

Petty offences for which women were summonsed included failing to whitewash walls, neglecting to sweep in front of their premises and various offences against liquor licenses. Nursemaids were frequently charged with breaching Hastings' bylaws by 'driving' perambulators on the pavement. The shilling fine was customarily paid by the employer.

The laws relating to coverture meant that a husband became liable for his wife's debts and contracts. A business owned by a married woman belonged in law to her husband. It led to some ludicrous situations. For example in 1864 Mr. Brockwell was fined £1 plus 13s costs because his wife had failed to register her business.[2]

A judge could overrule coverture if he felt so inclined and had good cause. Shopkeeper Mrs. Jane Foster of 104 All Saints' Street was sued by her greengrocery supplier for a debt of £8. She pleaded coverture; however after being subjected to a 'searching cross-examination' by the plaintiff's counsel she admitted to having a sexual relationship for eight years with her lodger. The Judge then stopped the case and said that a woman living in adultery could not claim coverture.[3]

Hastings gaol was a five-storey, brick building in the Bourne with a small triangular yard in front, surrounded on all sides by streets. The site is now covered by the tarmac of the A259 adjacent to the *King's Head*. There were separate day rooms for each sex, seven cells for men with three beds in each and one cell for women, measuring 14ft x 7ft and containing three beds. Women comprised 15% of the inmates of the gaol in 1850. The table overleaf shows the types of crime and the punishments meted out. Of the

FEMALES IN HASTINGS GAOL IN 1850

Name	Age	Offence	Sentence
Elizabeth Meek	31	Misbehaviour in the workhouse	14 days hard labour
Esther Brooker	34	Vagrancy	7 days hard labour
Ann Ellis	32	Uttering forged & counterfeit coin	Discharged
Elizabeth Easton	45	Assault	Fined
Harriet Miller	30	Vagrancy	7 days hard labour
Henrietta White	13	Larceny (i.e. theft)	1 month hard labour
Ann Blackman	25	Larceny (previous conviction)	Discharged
Martha Veness	30	Wilful damage	Fined
Catherine Egan	53	Larceny (prev. conv.)	8 months hard labour partly solitary
Elizab.Uptaine	20	Vagrancy (prev.conv.)	7 days hard labour
Mary Moon	37	Larceny (prev. conv.)	6 weeks hard labour
Caroline Upton	18	Vagrancy (2 prev. conv.)	1 month hard labour
Georgiana Palmer	13	Assault	14 days
Charlotte Payne	40	Larceny	3 months hard labour partly solitary.
Martha Veniss	30	Assault (prev. conv.)	Fined
Sarah Kent	52	Assault	10 days
Elizab. Windser	17	Larceny	2 months hard labour partly solitary.
Harriet Beale	16	Rogue and Vagabond	14 days
Jane Tollhurst	53	Assault	Fined

114

eighteen women inmates, half could neither read nor write. The list includes only local residents and omits the 19 travellers also incarcerated that year.[4]

A surprising number of Hastings women appeared in court charged with assaulting their husbands. One of them, Frances Gearing, was habitually beaten by her husband James, a fish-dealer, but when she hit back she was summonsed for assault. James called her 'a disgrace to her sex' because she failed to look after their five children, preferring to stay out to all hours in the company of men and prostitutes. One night she became drunk and used 'expressions such as are not fit for any woman to utter', threw a piece of broken plate and a tea-tin at him and threatened to burn down the rope-shop in which he sought refuge, and to kill him. She received a month's imprisonment.[5]

Among the commonest crimes of women was stealing. Servants had endless opportunities to steal from employers, as did lodgers from landladies. The usual routine was to pawn stolen goods for cash. Detection was remarkably easy since the pawnbroker could identify the thief. Punishments for theft were extraordinarily severe by today's standards but were much lighter than those meted out in the 18th century when, for example, for stealing handkerchiefs worth 10d Ann Colbran was ordered to be 'stript from the Waist upwards' and 'whipt till her back be bloody' at the public whipping post in the Bourne.[6] Fifty years later transportation to the colonies was the punishment for theft. In 1825 Mrs. Anne White was sentenced to seven years' transportation for obtaining by deception three packs of playing cards worth 15s from George Wooll of 5 High Street. She pretended that they were for some ladies at 2 The Croft. This type of crime was common throughout the century because shopkeepers routinely allowed goods to be taken by servants on approval and later added the items to the householder's account. In 1827 a thief called Eliza Dean was transported for seven years. She was sent to the convict ship *Louisa* at Woolwich with a wardrobe of new clothes that cost Hastings ratepayers £2. 12s 6d. It comprised:

1 new cotton jacket or gown
1 new cotton petticoat
2 new flannel petticoats
3 new shifts
2 new neckerchiefs coloured
2 pairs of shoes
3 pairs stockings of which 2 worsted

Two more Hastings women - Ann Blackman and Sarah Smith - were sentenced to transportation in 1852 and 1853. Some convict ships ('hulks') were used as prisons and did not, in fact, leave for the colonies. Conditions on board were harsh, primitive and rat-infested. Boys up to six and girls up to ten were allowed to accompany transported mothers but no woman could be transported if she had a child at her breast.[7]

Transportation was abolished in 1867, but from the early 1860s long custodial sentences took its place. Laundress Ann Penhall received eight months hard labour when she tried to pawn two stolen tablecloths and

FEMININE PUGNACITY.—*Louisa Thomas* (21), a prostitute, was charged as follows :—P.C. Henry Voke saw the prisoner about eleven the night before with her bonnet and jacket off fighting another female. She was also making use of very bad language. He took her into custody, and "conveyed" her to the station—that was he had to drag her. She kicked and bit on the road. She got his finger into her mouth, but he "did not leave it there long enough for her to bite it." He didn't charge her at the station with an assault as she did not hurt him much.—In reply to the prisoner the constable admitted he tore her sleeve out of her frock, but it was done in consequence of her resistance. — There had been a previous conviction against the prisoner for the same offence, for which she suffered one month's hard labour.—She was now fined 10s. and costs.

Below Publisher Thomas Brett enjoyed penning silly verses about magistrates' court cases. This one relates to a prostitute stealing from a client. *Brett's St Leonards & Hastings Gazette, 24 February 1872.*

PAINS, PENALTIES & PARAGRAMS.
(*Hastings Police Court.*)

NOTE-ABILITY.

[Ann Watson committed for trial on a charge of stealing a £5 note from James Hinckley.]

James Hinckley, sailor-youth, R.N., who goes to war's alarms, was seen with women and with men, to drink at Druids' Arms. One woman of immoral fame, who walks about the street, and with Ann Watson for her name, bade sailor-boy "stand treat." Young Hinckley then was nothing loth, so pulled out many a pound ; and, sailor-like, too fond of broth, he gave them glasses round. He paid for what the treating cost, from pocket at his breast ; and, lest his money should be lost, he then replaced the rest. Amongst that money was a note for five full sterling pounds ; and Watson's eyes perchance did gloat to get it out of bounds. With arm around the sailor's neck, with hand upon his breast, Ann Watson did her man attack, that is, she him caressed. He pushed aside, and she went out ; he would not have her fawn ; but soon, alas ! it came about, his five-pound note was gone. It was not long ere note was traced to Hinckley's would-be pal, nor long before at Court was placed that very *nice young gal*. Enough was known, enough was shown to place in durance vile this loving lass, as frail as glass, henceforth to take her trial.

a pair of drawers, while Lowannah Potten served nine months for stealing some items of cheap clothing. For stealing a veil and dress from her father in 1860, 19-year-old Frances Ashton was given three months with hard labour and Maria Sargent, aged 56, served six weeks hard labour with ten days in solitary confinement for stealing a shift worth a shilling.

Although prostitution itself was not illegal the activities of 'unfortunates', as they were euphemistically called, landed them in court repeatedly. The statistics for 1872 also reveal that 16% of all women arrested were known to be prostitutes. About half of their offences were drink-related; sleeping out, brawling and robbery made up the rest.[8] They would have a few gins or beers (drunk and disorderly); accost men in the street (obstruction); tell them in graphic terms what was on offer (using obscene language); sometimes collapse in the street (drunk and incapable); and, if they had no bed for the night, they crawled into a hut, shed or boat (sleeping out).

Theft and prostitution went together well. Men, stupefied with alcohol and distracted by lust were often mugged. Among the many culprits were Ann Watson, who stole £5 from a sailor with whom she was doing 'business', and Ann Chainey, who robbed a punter of 5s. Both served six months with hard labour. More seriously, Julia Davis teamed up with her live-in lover - a seaman - to assault and rob a tipsy young carpenter of £7.10s in John Street, for which they each received a year's penal servitude.

In 1833, the Poor Law Commissioners for Sussex described beer-shops as 'most mischievous', because they 'allow of secret meetings' and were run by 'the lowest class of persons'. It added that they were 'receiving houses for stolen goods, and frequently brothels'.[9] In 1856 Sarah Huggett's beer-shop, *The Mackeral,* was described by Inspector Battersby as 'a brothel of the worst description'. Sarah collaborated with Elizabeth Midgley, - 'a prostitute of the worst class', - to rob working-men who wanted lodgings. They would get a man drunk, undress him and put him into bed with Midgley. During these proceedings anything of value was found and filched. They were caught when a soldier complained of being divested of £3. 5s and a silver watch. In court, Midgley admitted taking the money and she received four months hard labour at Lewes, while Huggett received only a caution about the bad conduct of *The Mackeral.*[10]

One night in 1867, Harry Cotton, a printer, collected a parcel of meat and suet he had earlier left with a pub landlady for safe keeping, and began to make his way home at about midnight. In George Street he met prostitute Mary Roberts and, after treating her to some gin and ale, she took him to her upstairs front room at 3 Henry Terrace, All Saints' Street. At about 2am Harry got up to leave, and found his parcel missing. Mary tried to persuade him that he'd left it in the pub, but he fetched a policemen and together they found it in an adjoining room. Mary claimed that he had given it to her, for them both to share the next day; however, magistrates did not believe her and she was sentenced to six weeks' hard labour.[11] Three years later Mary was again prosecuted, this time for being drunk and obstructing the pavement.

117

SERIOUS CHARGE AND VERDICT OF MANSLAUGHTER AGAINST A SERVANT.

We are sorry to be called upon to record the perpetration of a crime of an unnatural character, in one of the most respectable parts of this usually quiet and orderly borough. The facts of the case are shortly these:—A female servant at No. 4, Carlisle parade, named Caroline Martin (and who was unknown to have been *enciente* until two days previously), was delivered of a female child early on the morning of Friday last. When her condition became known, surgical assistance was obtained, and it was found the mother had placed the infant in a common clothes box. The babe was rescued from death by suffocation; but there is reason to suppose that its unnatural parent had endeavoured to deprive it of life previously by strangulation and also by forcing some object—suspicion pointing to a piece of steel hoop, such as is used for the purpose of expanding a certain article of feminine apparel—down the little innocent's throat, which produced two wounds, and no doubt was the ultimate cause of death.

The case of Caroline Martin, which provoked a passionate outburst from a reader of the local press, incensed at the injustice to women (see p.123).

Attempting suicide was a crime in the 19th century. In 1872 prostitute Mary Elliott was sent to prison for seven days after being dragged out of the sea at the west end of George Street. Charlotte Nickerson, aged just 15,[12] tried to kill herself in 1860 after being seduced, made pregnant and abandoned by James Douglas.[13] Suicide was much more prevalent among men; however, women greatly outnumbered men as killers. In the mid-19th century two local women killed their husbands and a large but unknown number killed their children.

Mary Ann Geering, née Plumb, was born at Westfield around 1800, the daughter of agricultural labourers. She went into domestic service and became pregnant by a farmhand while still a teenager. After a forced marriage at Westfield Church, they set up home at Guestling. The couple had eight children during their 30-year marriage. They were both volatile people and were always arguing. Mary found it difficult to submit to a husband's authority and once asserted 'no man will rule me!' After many years of poverty, frustration, violence and unhappiness Mary subjected her husband to repeated arsenical poisoning until she had killed him. Thought to be a victim of heart disease, he was buried without a post-mortem. Mary applied for the appropriate sickness and death benefits from the Guestling Friendly Society, and proceeded to carry out the same procedure on her 21 year old son, then on his 26 year old brother. After their deaths, she turned her attention to her 18 year old son. Frederic Ticehurst, the surgeon treating him, became suspicious and had the boy removed from his mother's care, whereupon he recovered. The police and coroner were notified, the three bodies were exhumed, and Mary was arrested. A 'quiet looking country woman', she claimed to be 'as innocent as my Almighty Creator' when indicted on three counts of murder and one of attempted murder. She was, however, found guilty and she confessed her crimes before being executed at Lewes in 1849 before a crowd of 4,000 people.[14]

In 1853 Sarah Smith (née Taught) stabbed her husband with a broken cheese knife during a drunken quarrel in their squalid room in Harold Mews behind the *Horse and Groom* in Mercatoria, St Leonards. She was sentenced to 10 years' transportation; however, due to her ill-health the Secretary of State agreed to let her stay at Lewes Gaol infirmary until she was well enough to make the journey. She died there in 1854.

The most common serious crime of women was the murder of unwanted babies. Infanticide was a massive problem in all parts of Victorian Britain and was a capital crime until 1938. Having an illegitimate child so devastated the lives of unmarried women that many thousands committed horrific acts out of sheer desperation. On finding themselves pregnant, some managed to hide the pregnancy and the birth, and then abandoned, exposed or killed with their own hands the new-born child.

Unmarried housemaid Hannah Moore became pregnant in February 1851 while in the service of the Duchess of St Albans at 5 Grand Parade, St Leonards, but within months she became housemaid to the Reverend William Gordon, of St Andrew's Presbyterian Church, West Hill Road.[15] The child was born on 15th November and on 28th a coroner's jury of 18 men viewed its body at Mercatoria police station. Later, at the *South*

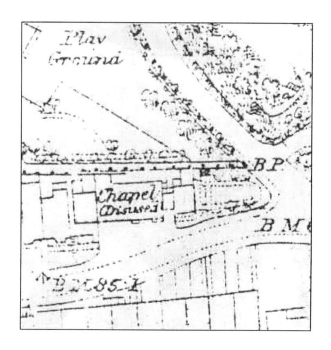

The Hannah Moore infanticide case.

Above: Map showing the site of the Presbyterian chapel at West Hill Road St Leonards, now covered by Hastings College.

Left: Victoria Passage, showing the back garden of 6 North St. In 1851, two tiny cottages infilled this garden and the privy was shared by all three homes. Hannah murdered her baby and, hiding it beneath her cloak, carried it to this passage and hid it in the privy.

Saxon Hotel, 13 Grand Parade, the jury heard from 16-year-old Catherine Pulford, of 6 North Street, who had found a mysterious bundle in the privy in her back yard. The yard gate opened into Victoria Passage which led to Shepherd Street. After trying to lift the bundle with laundry-tongs, her grandfather called extra-constable Barnes of 9 Lavatoria who tucked up his shirt sleeves and pulled out the body of a baby, wrapped in an apron, with a glass cloth and some thread twisted tightly round its neck.

As news of the discovery emerged a local doctor, Roger Gardiner of 51 Marina, recalled a consultation with Hannah Moore in May when she was three months pregnant and had wanted to terminate the pregnancy. He said, 'She wished me to give her some stronger medicine which from my suspicions I did not do.' Jane Lamb of 2 Victoria Passage, the chapel cleaner, saw Hannah in bed on 15th with blood on the floor. Jane's neighbour Anna Ashdown told how she had met Hannah in Victoria Passage on the 19th, wearing a plaid cloak and appearing very stout. Hannah asked to use a privy and Anna had shown her to the one behind 6 North Street. After denying everything Hannah submitted to a doctor's examination in the presence of the cook. She then admitted that labour began at 3am, but she worked until 1pm. She then gave birth in her room at 1.30, bound a cloth around the child's mouth, strangled it with thread, wrapped it in her apron and hid it in a box under the bed. She placed the afterbirth in the water-closet and returned to her duties. Over the weekend the cook, Sarah Dowker, shared a bedroom with Hannah but suspected nothing. Four days later Hannah took the infant's body to Victoria Passage and hid it inside the Pulford's privy. While awaiting trial Hannah told her nurse - Mary Ann Miller, of 8 Shepherd Street - that she had not intended to kill the baby. 'but by some irresistible impulse she couldn't help it'.

The jury returned a verdict of wilful murder and Hannah was sent for trial at Lewes Assizes. She was so ill that she was held in the gaol infirmary until March 1852. At the trial she pleaded not guilty. Her age, given as 30 in the April 1851 Census, and 28 in the November 1851 newspaper, dropped to 24 at the start of the trial and to 23 by the end of it. Presumably her counsel believed youth to be an advantage. The jury found her guilty of murder but the judge ordered them to reconsider. The men debated for a further 50 minutes before returning a verdict of 'guilty of concealment of birth' but 'not guilty of wilful murder' since they were 'not certain of the prisoner being in complete possession of her faculties at the time.' She was sentenced to two years' hard labour. This sentence was incredibly lenient. In a similar case in Surrey in 1859 a 19 year old who was made pregnant through rape was sentenced to death for infanticide.

Hannah Moore was one of the few Hastings women who were caught. Others included Sarah Judge, aged 17, who murdered her unwanted baby in 1852 by cutting its throat with scissors. In 1860 Caroline Martin, a domestic servant, did 'feloniously kill and slay her infant female bastard child' at 4 Carlisle Parade. After secretly giving birth in her employer's house she put the baby in her wooden servant's box at the foot of her bed. Another servant heard gurgling and although found alive the child later died. Caroline was found guilty of wilful murder.

While juries did not condone infanticide, many sympathised with the women's desperation and were reluctant to return verdicts of murder, because of the extreme sentences judges would be compelled to give. In 1860 Mary Ann Looker, resident cook at 79 Marina, gave birth in secret. She wrapped the baby in muslin, placed it in a small wicker basket and put that into her carpet-bag in the servant's hall. It lay undiscovered for a fortnight. Thomas Brett[16] had the misfortune to be foreman of the jury that viewed the corpse, which was in 'a most unpleasant state'.[17] But Looker was found guilty only of concealment of birth, because the coroner accepted her claim that the baby was still-born. She died while awaiting trial. In 1858 members of the public submitted a petition pleading for a lenient sentence to be given to Emma Sutton, then awaiting trial for concealing the birth of her illegitimate child. Their grounds were threefold: her extreme youth, her lack of a mother and because she had been too overcome with tears to offer any defence. She was sentenced to six months hard labour.[18] In 1861 servant Eliza Thomas of 6 Castledown Avenue killed her baby and hid it in her servants' box, nailing down the lid. She then left her employer and returned to her family home. By the time the body was found it was impossible for the coroner's jury to return any verdict other than 'found dead.' Eliza escaped with just one month in prison for concealment of birth. The following year a laundress at Cliff Cottage, West Hill Road, exposed her baby and let it die but, again, the coroner had insufficient evidence to prove it was born alive and no charges were brought. In 1865 servant Ellen Cornford, of 58 George Street, killed her newborn child, wrapped it in the sleeve of a black alpaca dress and dumped it in West Street. The surgeon deposed that the child had breathed, and an alpaca dress with a sleeve missing was found in Ellen's possession, but she was charged only with concealment of birth and unlawfully disposing of an illegitimate child, and was sentenced to just one week in prison.

An average of two infants a year were found abandoned in Hastings & St Leonards - a shocking statistic for two such small towns. There were surely many more that remained undiscovered. The newspaper reports were relentless: in 1858 one was found in a well in St Leonards; in 1859 two were left on the beach within a few weeks of each other a third was discovered in Eft Pond on the West Hill; a fourth - a well-dressed and well-nourished 3 month old boy - was found 40ft down a well at the rear of 7 Cross Street. At this point the coroner announced with considerable concern that this was the sixth such case in just 18 months - then another was washed up on the beach opposite Pelham Place. Yet another was discovered in a basket in a hedge in Deudney's field and, as it was clearly murder, a £50 reward was offered - with no result. During the winter of 1860, one was found frozen on the path from Tackleway to the East Hill. In 1863 one newborn was found hidden behind a toilet seat in Hastings station while another was found drowned in a stream at the bottom of Newgate Wood, sewn neatly and tightly into a dress-lining. A third was found by a gate leading to the rear of 11 Magdalen Road. The marks on its neck and 'other indications of unnatural treatment' led the coroner's jury to return a verdict of 'wilful murder' but in most cases the child was said to have been 'found dead' even when it was likely that it did not die from natural causes. At an 1864 inquest into the death of an infant found by a beach scavenger in a WC near the Fishermen's Church, the surgeon could not say whether or not the child had breathed. The coroner advised the jury that if they decided the child was still-born the case could be closed. The jury swiftly obliged with the desired verdict.[19] In 1866 one baby girl was found strangled on the Castle rocks while another was found in a hedge in Stonefield Road wrapped in a copy of the *Daily Telegraph*.

The discovery of unwanted dead infants was so common all over Britain that an Act was passed in 1867 ordering that they must be conveyed to the nearest public house and the Secretary of State offered a £50 reward for information leading to the arrest of the women responsible. If found, a woman was delivered into the hands of men as jurors, magistrates, surgeons, counsel and judges, who asked no questions about the father of the child. This state of affairs incensed an anonymous correspondent to the *Hastings & St Leonards News* who in 1860, prompted by the case of the aforementioned Caroline Martin, wrote:

> ... neither in this case nor in any of the undiscovered ones - have I heard the query *"Who is the father of the child?"* and yet this is a most important question; for I do not I cannot believe that any woman in this country would destroy her infant ... if she had the sympathy and support of the father of the child.
>
> It is because he is a sneak and a coward - because *he* is so mean as to leave her to her trouble - so selfishly debauched as to care only for the gratification of his own passions - so cowardly as to shirk any part of the burden - so dastardly as to add *his* contempt to that of the world - it is because of this that such murders do take place; and therefore *whoever* the father of any such "slaughtered innocent" may be he is not only a villain and coward but *accessory* to the murder; as *he* and mark you he only might have prevented it.
>
> A striking contrast to this cowardice is the courage so constantly exhibited by women who have been convicted of infanticide. Without exposing or even naming those whose villainy has made them criminals - without trying to include them in the crime (though probably the crime has been *suggested* by the man) - without uttering a complaint against *them* - these have borne the trial, the contumely, the punishment, in silence ...
>
> It is an hypocritical mockery to talk severely of child-murder *while* the partner of the first crime goes unscathed. It is adding injustice to misery to punish *that* severely *until* society demands vigorously chastity in men as well as chastity in women. [20] (Original emphasis)

The usual punishment for infanticide was four years' imprisonment, a ruined reputation, and severely limited employment prospects, which drove many women into prostitution. In 1860 Police Superintendent Glenister opined:

123

INDECENT ASSAULT.— A SALUTARY PUNISHMENT.— *William Earle*, an errand boy of fifteen, living in Norman road, was charged, on a warrant, with indecently assaulting Jane Goodsell, a servant-girl of seventeen.

Complainant and prisoner were both in the employ of a tradesman in the South Colonnade, St. Leonards, respectively as servant and errand boy. On Thursday evening, about nine o'clock, the girl was sent to the Post Office (Mr. Southall's). When near the west end of the Colonnade, she was met by the prisoner (and nearly a dozen others, of about his own age), who came towards her and took indecent liberties with her clothing. She expostulated with him, and then the whole lot "set at her" and knocked her down on the pavement. Other indignities (which are unfit for publication) were inflicted upon her, and she then got away from them. Not content with having committed one offence, the mischievous rascals met her again, on her return, and repeated a similar outrage. Prisoner (who had been picked out because he was foremost, and also because he was the only one known) had also made use of a disgustingly obscene threat towards complainant, in her master's kitchen, on the previous Monday evening.

Mary Ann Brett, another servant girl, living on the Marina, who had accompanied complainant to the Post Office and back, and had witnessed both assaults, fully corroborated the evidence previously given.

Prisoner said he had nothing to say. He did not deny the charge.

Fined 40s. and costs ; in default, one month's imprisonment.

The Mayor expressed a hope that the punishment would be a warning, both to prisoner and to his companions, not to be engaged in such outrageous conduct in future.

> If this most serious crime were more severely punished it would be of less frequent occurrence and I do not think that the sympathy of some (perhaps well-meaning) persons towards offenders of this class has a good effect upon those who are likely to commit such a crime.[21]

His advice was not heeded; on the contrary, punishments seem to have become lighter, judging by two cases from 1874. In the first Jane Furner, a 19-year-old cook at 14 Markwick Terrace, killed her newborn boy and locked his body in her servant's box in her attic room. Local magistrates, having heard the surgeon's evidence that 'he had not the slightest doubt' that the child was born alive and had been strangled, found her guilty of wilful murder. The second case was almost identical: Keturah Holter, aged 35, a domestic servant at 2 Warrior Square, admitted strangling her newborn child with an apron string and hiding the body in a drawer. She too was found guilty of murder. Both women were sent for trial at Lewes Assizes where, amazingly, both were cleared of the murders they had openly admitted, and found guilty only of the lesser offence of concealment of birth, for which they served sentences of just a few months each.

Crimes against women

The commonest crime committed against well-off women was theft, either by burglary or, more often, by their domestic servants. The most common crime against poor women was assault by their husbands. Violence was common in Victorian marriages, particularly among the working classes, where drunkenness played its part and social niceties were lacking. In cases of habitual violence a wife could apply to the magistrates and her husband could be bound over on a bail of £20 for six months. If he reoffended in that period he would be sent to gaol.

One cause of marital strife was the use of prostitutes. Many wives became jealous and angry about the time and money husbands spent on 'street-girls' while neglecting their families. Magistrates, ideologically supporting the family, took the wives' side. At the *Queen's Head Inn*, Fishmarket, in 1864 prostitute Ann Taster was viciously attacked by Ann Casey, sustaining two black eyes and a swollen face. When magistrates heard that the victim had spent the afternoon consorting with the defendant's husband, he fined the latter just 5s, because she had suffered such 'great provocation'.[22] In 1859 George Money, a travelling harp-player living at the *Derby Arms*, Union St, was arrested for assaulting his wife Elizabeth. George had brought a prostitute home and ordered his wife to pretend he was a single man. When she refused he struck her in the face leaving her with a black eye and covered in blood from her nose and mouth. Walking out, he left his wife without money or food. The couple lived in abject poverty but, when arrested, George was treating two prostitutes to a meal out. The two girls waited outside during George's court hearing but he received two months' hard labour. The Mayor, calling the assault 'disgraceful and unprovoked', took pity on Elizabeth and gave her 2/6d out of the Poor Box, remarking that she was 'a deserving object'. [23]

Maria Taught refused to cohabit with her fisherman husband because he used prostitutes. She slept with the children. One night he rolled in at midnight, drunk, and ordered her to go to bed with him, which she refused. He threw her bedclothes on the floor and threatened to throw her and the children out of doors 'as he had before'. Seizing Maria by the hair he dragged her out of bed, smashing her head against a wooden box, and dragged her round the room by the arm and hair, striking her several times while she screamed and struggled. He smothered her screams with a pillow, tore off her night-dress, spat in her face and raped her. She sued for assault. The magistrate was shown a night-dress torn to shreds, and a great clump of hair that Taught had wrenched from his wife's head. He expressed disbelief that three hours of screaming brought no assistance but a neighbour gave evidence that he had heard 'scuffling' for a considerable time. Taught claimed that Maria had 'drunken and idle habits' prompting the magistrate to remark that there were 'faults on both sides'. Taught was fined just 5 shillings plus costs.

The laws relating to coverture meant that if a crime was committed against a married woman only her husband could prosecute. When lodging house keeper Esther Nash had some hair combs and stockings stolen by her young servant in 1851, her husband was named in court as the victim even though only Mrs. Nash and the accused woman attended court.[24] The husband of Mrs. May, a grocer, had to sue for a debt incurred by one of her customers in 1861. In 1870 Mrs. Croft, landlady of the *Bohemia Arms,* wished to sue Henry Towner for slander. He had boasted loudly in the *Plasterer's Arms,* Cross Street, that he had slept with her. But only Mr. Croft could sue, which he did, winning £25 damages. No matter how serious the crime, a married woman could not sue. In 1849 railwayman John Storey raped 'the wife of Mr. Frederick Whyborn' in a railway carriage. According to the law it was Mr. Whyborn's 'property' that sustained the damage and the decision to prosecute was his alone. Storey was fined £1 with 17s 6d costs.[25]

Homicide was very rare and, as we have seen, the most common were infanticides committed by women. Brett alluded briefly to the murder of a prostitute that happened about 1834 at the rear of the *Albion Hotel* in George Street. This was memorialised in a verse:

> In a timber-yard of Ball's - now Albion Mews
> One "Mud-Jack's" wife some brute did badly use
> Whose lifeless form as seen by morning light
> Had undergone ill treatment in the night
> A fallen creature was that "Mud Jack's" wife
> Yet God alone should take away life.

One of the most shocking crimes of the mid-century was an assault on a 56-year-old cook, Jane Cannon, who had been in the service of the same family for 26 years. She was performing her duties at Catherine Villa,

West Hill Road, on 12th November 1848 while the family was at church. Burglars entered the house one of whom coshed Jane three times over the head. She died two days later. The murderer, Pearson, attended the service at St Clement's Church that evening and was arrested in the nearby *Hastings Arms* while supping beer.

Crimes against the person attracted lower fines and lighter sentences than theft. For example, in 1855 a man seen by two witnesses to indecently assault a four-year-old girl was fined 20 shillings or one month hard labour in default. In comparison, in 1852 Sarah Ann Burden, aged 18, served six weeks hard labour - the final week in solitary confinement - for stealing two pairs of boots.

In cases of a sexual nature women were often cleared from the courtroom, and the local press refused to publish any evidence of 'a disgusting nature'. In 1862 the Minister of the Croft Chapel was charged with several counts of rape; his victim was his 13-year-old servant. The court was crammed with what the local paper described as the 'Cream of the East End'.[26] It was a very important case with much local interest but the distressed child had to give her evidence without a single member of her sex present because all the women were ordered to leave court. Owing to the lack of witnesses (which, in a rape case, is not surprising) the charge was reduced to 'aggravated assault upon a female' and eventually the Minister was acquitted. These cases often resulted in light sentences or acquittals, provoking the editor of the *Hastings & St Leonards News* to declare:

> Magistrates and juries have a wonderful sympathy with many male … offenders and pass some strange sentences at times … when the evidence is strong enough to prove a criminal charge (of rape for instance) the jury prefer convicting on a lighter charge to avoid apparently the infliction of a heavier penalty. This is a false mercy to society as well as a gross injustice to the woman. The consequence is that beasts in the shape of men take less trouble to control their passions and violent assaults on women in defenceless circumstances are numerous enough to disgrace a country pretending to be civilised and religious. It would be well sometimes for jurymen to remember that they have wives daughters sisters and friends of their own … [27]

Women were permitted to hear the trial of William Wood, arrested for molesting three little girls in one week in 1860. As the girls were too young to identify Wood he was discharged. However when he left the Court he was followed by 'a crowd of the élite of the Fishmarket (feminine gender) who give him the credit of having previously occupied himself in an equally disgusting manner'.[28] Wood's fate at the hands of this mob of furious fishwives was, unfortunately, not recorded. Roger Kennet, a Bohemia butcher, sexually assaulted a seven-year-old and exposed himself to her nine-year-old sister. The girls in this instance being older, they were able to make a positive identification and he received six months hard labour - the maximum sentence.

The outcome of a case involving anything sexual depended on the perceived moral status of the victim. One St Leonards man was acquitted of rape the instant the court heard that the unmarried victim had not been a virgin at the time of the attack. In another case, a man who was 'annoying females by approaching them and uttering obscenities' was fined 15s. The magistrate remarked that 'it was bad enough to annoy unfortunate girls (prostitutes) in this manner but respectable women must be protected from such conduct.' [29]

REFERENCES

[1] Superintendent Glenister, *Annual Report of Statistics of Local Offices 1862-3*.

[2] *Hastings & St Leonards Chronicle* 8 June 1864.

[3] *Hastings & St Leonards News* 8 January 1864.

[4] *Hastings Gaol Records 1850-53. Keeper's Commitment Book*. PBN Publications 1993.

[5] *Hastings & St Leonards News* 14 April 1865

[6] Court Sessions Book.

[7] Hastings Gaol Records East Sussex Records Office.

[8] More information on prostitutes, and on hawkers of both sexes, is included in *Down and Out in Victorian Hastings*.

[9] Extracts from the 1833 Poor Law Commissioners Report

[10] *Hastings & St Leonards News* 23 April 1856

[11] *Hastings & St Leonards News* 27 April 1867

[12] The age of consent was then 12, it was raised to 13 in 1875, then to 16 in 1885. 13 in 1875, and then to 16 in 1885.

[13] *Hastings & St Leonards News* 20 April 1860

[14] *Hastings & St Leonards News* 27 April 1849.

[15] The site is now covered by Hastings College.

[16] A journalist and chronicler of Victorian Hastings.

[17] *Hastings & St Leonards News* 20 April 1860 and Brett T. B. *Histories* Volume 88 p.55

[18] Brett T. B. *Histories* Volume 7 p.78.

[19] *Hastings & St Leonards News* 17 June 1864

[20] *Hastings & St Leonards News* 4 April 1860.

[21] Annual Police Returns October 1860.

[22] *Hastings & St Leonards News* 1 January 1864.

[23] Magistrates' Court Report 24 September 1859

[24] *Hastings & St Leonards News*. 6 May 1851.

[25] *Hastings & St Leonards News* 20 October 1849.

[26] The eastern end of Hastings - the Old Town.

[27] *Hastings & St Leonards News* 21 August 1863

[28] *Hastings & St Leonards News* 27 May 1860

[29] *South Eastern Advertiser* 20 January 1872

Interesting Individuals

This short chapter contains features about some interesting, and some eccentric, women of mid-19th-century Hastings.

The Countess Of Waldegrave:
Hastings' greatest Victorian benefactress

Sarah, Countess Waldegrave wielded more influence upon mid-century Hastings than any other woman. Although she owned a London residence at 4 Harley Street, she was dedicated to Hastings and lived for 55 years in The Mansion, Old London Road (now Old Hastings House).

She was born in 1787, the daughter of the rector of St Clement's Church, the Reverend Whitear, at Hastings Old Town Rectory, 106 High Street. Aged 30, she was married at All Soul's Church, Langham Place, London, to Edward Milward Junior, twenty times Mayor of Hastings. Such was their social standing that the Bishop of Chichester conducted the service. On Milward's death in 1833 she inherited a life interest in his great wealth, which included the West and East hills, Fishponds Farm, which extended beyond Fairlight Glen and the Lovers' Seat, as well as much property including some at Westfield, Guestling and Pett. Sarah had no children but after 13 years of widowhood she married William, the 8th Earl Waldegrave, who had seven children from a previous marriage. He died in 1859 and Sarah remained a widow for the remainder of her days.

The Countess is best remembered for laying the foundation stones of ten churches which she endowed.[1] The first was at Halton in 1838, for which she donated the church and parsonage, the site, and even the building stone. She founded schools for St Clement's and All Saints' parishes and gave both land and funds to build Halton School, and donated £500 for an infants' school and a house for the mistress. She financed numerous Sunday schools, poor-schools and institutions, and provided wash houses and public baths in Bourne Street for the impoverished inhabitants of the Old Town.

She paid for a Fisherman's Institute in All Saints' Street and was involved in the Hastings Literary and Scientific Institution. She bought uniforms and a rifle range at Ecclesbourne for the Volunteer Rifle Corps, and built a Mission House in All Saints' School yard. She helped negotiate for, and donated £100 to secure, a Public Recreation Ground at Priory Meadow. She was a major donor to every appeal for funds for the victims of accidents, and for widows of fishermen lost at sea; indeed, her name is almost always found among the top five contributors. Organisers knew that once her patronage was secured, that of others would follow. Her name also headed a Memorial (i.e. petition) signed only by ladies and submitted to the Commissioners in 1861, opposing the building of an international harbour.

Among the signatories' fears were that an influx of sailors would increase prostitution and that the streets would no longer be safe for ladies.

Sarah was a great benefactor, but she enjoyed using her money to manipulate and control people. She was far from unique in this; recent historians have associated the charitable act with 'ambition, egotism, a desire for deference, and power-seeking [in] an attempt to create obligations to oneself which will enable one to exercise control over people.'[2] Sarah compelled people to do things her way by attaching strict conditions to her gifts. When she endowed All Saints' School on the East Hill with £100 in 1835, it was on condition that there were separate girls' and boys' entrances. She allowed public access to Ecclesbourne Glen and the Lovers' Seat only if no alcoholic beverage was sold there, because 'numbers of ladies stroll

about these heights and frequently without an escort, and it would not do for these gentle creatures to be liable on their return home to the rudeness and swilled insolence of late wassailers on the lonely downs or in the blind mazes of the tangled woods.'[3] She was conservative to the point of being a killjoy and used her privileged position to halt or prevent many kinds of revelry, including cricket and dancing parties on the East Hill. She once gave orders to close a well-used footpath, though to her annoyance she was forced to re-open it. T. B. Brett wrote:

In Eighteen-Thirty sev'n a path was stopped
Which present writer frequently had hopped,
And which said stoppage he – the right to try –
Did all the printed notices defy.

T'was Mrs. Milward's arbitrary act,
Which soon she found it prudent to retract.
If thou wouldst know where this pathway was found
It led from West-hill mills to Barrack-ground.[4]

The Countess disapproved of anything that strayed from her rigid, ultra-conservative point of view: nonconformists, dissenters, radicals, and reformers all received short shrift. She was against the women's rights movement and strongly opposed votes for women. However, she was deeply interested in educating native Indian women in domesticity and health, and allowed an Easter 'tabletop sale' to take place in her drawing room to raise funds for them. At the consecration of St John's Church, Hollington, she gave an impromptu speech against the 'ritualistic' – that is, Roman Catholic - practices that were taking place at Christ Church, one of the few churches not endowed by her. While visiting a girls' school on Cumberland in 1867 she lectured them on the evils of 'loving finery' and dressing up, warning that their future employers would not like it. The speech was conveyed to Hastings girls by way of the local newspaper. The Countess' fabulous wealth could have bought vast amounts of finery yet she chose to present 'a pattern of neatness and simplicity in her attire'.

Countess Waldegrave was a woman sometimes disliked and feared, but always respected, by local clergymen, councillors and other officials with whom she dealt. They seem to have cowered in deference during their dealings with her; her title, wealth and their obligation to show immense gratitude on behalf of the poor and the Church of England made it impossible for them to show their true feelings. Nor did her family nurse any great affection for her: the MP's daughter Catherine North considered it a close escape that the Countess did not give her away at her wedding, having threatened to do so. She still gave the first speech at the wedding breakfast. One gets the impression of an overbearing woman who habitually muscled in where she was not wanted.

As a businesswoman, she was shrewd. During the planning of St Andrew's Square and Queen's Road in 1862, the Countess donated to the Council a strip of unused land near the gas works, retaining the strips each side of it. In return she exacted from the officials a seemingly strange condition – that they must continue to build Queen's Road in a straight line. The Council agreed, and gave its heartfelt thanks for her generosity. Once the Council had financed the road construction, using her strip of ground, the Countess sold her plots of land on each side of the newly made-up road for £6,250 – a very tidy sum in those days.

Over a 40-year period the Countess assisted in treats and outings for thousands of children at All Saints' and St Clement's schools. In 1856, 118 pupils, 'being anxious to testify their gratitude', spent many weeks collecting subscriptions amongst themselves to present her with a gift: a cottage tea urn. Four years later, £200 was collected from the townspeople, including pennies from children educated at the various schools she had endowed, to erect a drinking fountain in her honour. It was an eighteen-feet high, Gothic confection, of Portland stone, with a groyned canopy supported by four marble columns. In the middle is Jesus with the Woman of Samaria, with an Evangelist at each of the four corners. Above are richly carved, crocketted finials. This was built in 1861 and erected outside Holy Trinity Church, Hastings; wealthy philanthropist Miss Sayer laid the first stone. At the unveiling ceremony the 74-year-old Countess was invited formally to open the fountain. She read out a prepared speech and took the first drink of water – via a glass - from one of the three jets.

Just four years later, the fountain was no longer operative. John Bazalgette[5] called it 'one of the prettiest drinking fountains in England' and opined that he knew 'nothing to compare to it for architectural beauty and good taste'; however, he continued,

> Its condition, as I have seen it, is disgraceful. It is dirty, and, unfortunately, in its state of dirt, IT IS DRY... devoid of that source of health it was intended to convey, in order to relieve the poor man from

the compulsion to visit the public-house and its consequent drunkenness.[6]

In 1873, the Countess died at The Mansion and was interred at Fairlight, where the Earl had been laid to rest in 1859. There is a memorial to them in the east window, south aisle, of St Clement's Church and several tablets commemorating the births and deaths of the Milwards and Waldegraves. A booklet has been published about the fountain, but not about the Countess.

The Waldegrave Drinking Fountain outside Holy Trinity Church, now a Grade II listed building: currently dilapidated, crumbling, - and dry!

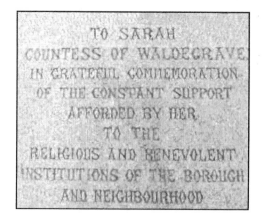

TO SARAH
COUNTESS OF WALDEGRAVE
IN GRATEFUL COMMEMORATION
OF THE CONSTANT SUPPORT
AFFORDED BY HER
TO THE
RELIGIOUS AND BENEVOLENT
INSTITUTIONS OF THE BOROUGH
AND NEIGHBOURHOOD

The Mackay Sisters:
Archetypal Victorian spinsters.

The Mackays were typical of the upper-class St Leonards residents of the mid-19th century. Lucy Mackay, a widow, of Bagthorpe Hall, Norfolk, and her three spinster daughters visited St Leonards from around 1832, staying in lodgings at Marina, and at West Hill Road, until they settled permanently in about 1840. The girls - Eliza, Emma and Charlotte - were 40, 45 and 48 in the 1841 Census. Their brother, Captain Henry Fowler Mackay, was the first Chief Constable of the East Sussex Constabulary.[7] His appointment in 1840 probably influenced their decision to settle in Sussex.

The Mackays were friends of James Burton, founder of St Leonards. During the town's infancy they helped set up many of its institutions and societies and contributed to collections for all kinds of enterprises, from new churches to soup kitchens; they also donated £3 towards extending West Hill Road westwards to the railway station. As befitted ladies of their station, the Mackays' were involved in charity work. In the 1840s they contributed generously to St Leonards' schools, the Infirmary and the Mendicity Society, and helped set up and run several charitable organisations, including clothing and coal clubs, which Eliza ran for almost 50 years. She was also treasurer of the Lying-In Society for Poor Married Women.

When a public appeal was opened for a new church their names were almost at the top of the list. They each gave a cash donation plus a promise (trust fund) to pay a yearly sum. The church was to be dedicated to St Mary Magdalen and it would have 850 seats, of which 450 were to be forever free of charge and for the exclusive use of the poor.[8] It opened in 1852. The sisters were also associated with the new Church of St Matthew, at Tivoli, and Eliza attended the ceremony of laying the foundation stone.

All four siblings engaged in archery. They became acquainted with Princess Victoria when she visited the town in 1834[9] and were probably responsible for persuading her to be patron of the Society of St Leonards Archers, which they had co-founded in 1833. Perhaps they were the instigators of a request, which Victoria granted, to change the name to The Queen's St Leonards Archers. Eliza and Charlotte were particularly enthusiastic toxophilites and were fiercely competitive. In a glittering career spanning three decades, between them the sisters won an enormous number of prizes[10] and would have won more had they not been given a handicap. In 1849, a local paper recorded that 'the shooting of the Misses Mackay is subject to ... deduction, or they would almost certainly bear away all the prizes'.[11] Emma enjoyed attending the rifle fêtes that started in 1852 at Halton, although no lady was permitted to compete.

Keen horticulturists, the Mackays also planned, ornamented, improved and maintained the archery grounds, which Burton had donated for the purpose, making them among the best in Britain. They also won several prizes at local horticulture shows.

133

ARCHERY MEETING.

The bye-meeting arranged for Saturday last, in order to shoot for the prizes annually given by P. F. Robertson, Esq., the President, was attended with unusual success. The day was favourable, the morning having been very brilliant; this, combined with the popularity of the donor, and the value of the prizes, tended to secure not only more than an average attendance of visitors, but a number of competitors very nearly equal to that of the grand annual meeting.

The prizes were six in number, articles of personal adornment for the fairer portion of humanity. The brooches were of silver, the central ornament consisting of a bunch of thistle-sprigs, gilt. Encircling the other ornamentation was engraved the legend, "St. Leonards-on-Sea Royal Archers." The prizes were much admired by numerous visitors, who had an opportunity of inspecting them. They were prepared specially for the occasion.

It is almost unnecessary to add that Herr Klee's band played a number of lively compositions throughout the afternoon; and that the grounds are in full luxuriance of summer vegetation. Upwards of four hours were occupied in shooting off the required number of arrows. At the close, the esteemed President, with his accustomed gallantry and good humour, presented the prizes to the following winners:

First prize,—Miss Mackay, whose score, in consequence of deductions made from some others, who had been prize winners at previous meetings, stood highest on the list. [Cries of "Bravo."]

134

The eldest, Eliza, was a lady of great social standing. Her name appears on the guest lists of all the society balls and other fashionable events. At one of the Brasseys' fancy dress balls she dressed as Countess Abergavenny. Such was her social eminence that she was invited to lay the first three bricks of the Priory Meadow railway tunnel on 24th July 1849.[12] This tunnel made it possible for the much needed and long-awaited railway to come into Hastings.

Mrs. Mackay died in 1849. She was 83, blind, and described as 'a pattern of piety.' Following a period of mourning, in 1854 her three daughters took a trip to the continent to do the Grand Tour and on their return they rented no. 1 Upland Views,[13] the first of six double-villas built on an elevated site overlooking the subscription gardens and the sea. A further five houses were being built and when the sixth and last, a nine-roomed villa, became ready in 1856 they bought it and engaged three residential domestic servants – a modest household compared with others. They enjoyed furnishing the house and laying out the gardens, and commissioned an extension to accommodate a billiard room, a very unusual feature in an all-female household. They hosted fancy-fairs in their beautiful garden to raise money for charity, and held society dinner-parties.

The youngest sister, Charlotte, died in 1862, aged 61, followed by Emma in 1869, aged 76, but Eliza stayed on in the large house until her death in 1885, aged 89. She retained two servants to the end, one of whom had lived and worked in her service for 31 years.

The Mackays home at the Uplands. The exterior of the house still retains its Victorian ambience and most of its original features. It is now a Grade II listed building.

Archery meeting at St Leonards in 1865 showing lady archers competing in crinolined skirts and corsets. Among this group is almost certainly the 70-year-old Eliza Mackay – but which lady is she?
Photograph reproduced by courtesy of Hastings Museum.

Elizabeth Breeds:
Eccentric extraordinaire

Details of the lifestyle of Elizabeth Breeds were known only to her close neighbours and kin, and are omitted from the written history of the Breeds family. Her father, Mark Breeds, was a prominent townsman; her brother, Robert Boykett Breeds, was an auctioneer and a highly respected figure in Hastings. He invited Elizabeth many times to live with him or with his daughter, who set up in business herself in 1856. Elizabeth always declined, preferring to live alone in the former family home in Guestling Village. Robert did everything he could for his sister: he purchased the house, paid the rates and sent her 10s a week.

Elizabeth lived in the scullery and slept in the kitchen, although there were four feather beds upstairs. She would not use the other rooms of the house. She refused to wear clothes; neighbours said she covered herself only with newspapers – some around her shoulders and others made up into an apron. When her two nieces visited they were shocked at her semi-nudity and had clothes sent to her immediately, which she promised to wear but never did. Elizabeth discharged her servant and became a recluse. She rarely if ever left the house; local people shopped for her, though she did not let them in. Robert became so worried about his dear sister that called a doctor to assess her. He pronounced her of sound mind, but merely eccentric.

One bitterly-cold day, in November 1859 a child, carrying out her daily duty by fetching Elizabeth a pail of water from the well, failed to obtain a reply despite repeatedly calling and knocking at the door. The alarm was raised and some local men broke in. They found Elizabeth lying on some cinders, dead. To their intense embarrassment, she was completely naked.

Officials described the kitchen as 'a heterogeneous mass of rubbish and disorder as it is almost impossible to conceive, - the things being mixed together and broken to pieces'. The coroner decided Elizabeth had died of debility owing to being cold.[14]

In a tragic sequel to Elizabeth's story, just two years later her brother Robert committed suicide by walking into the sea. Mrs. Ellen Berry ran into the water, caught hold of his hand and tried to pull him out. Hampered by her long skirts and the movement of the waves, this proved impossible; but she managed to catch his legs and lift them up onto the groyne to prevent him being washed away. It took five men to drag his body out. Mrs. Berry was recommended for an award from the Humane Society.

Caroline Carey:
Naïve artist ruthlessly exploited

Caroline Carey was born in 1817 of a wealthy father, but he made bad investments and lost his money, so Caroline became a governess in London. She later gained her independence through a legacy left by her grandmother, and purchased a lodging house in Hastings, despite having little talent for business. She appears to have been seized with enthusiasm for buying and letting houses and at one time had forty under her control, a fact which the casual reader of the 1862 street directory would not suspect from the entry: *Caroline Carey, 12 Magdalen Road, lodging house keeper.*

The houses were all in good situations and doing well but Caroline's talents were literary and artistic and not financial, so she found the book-keeping and accounts too much for her. The husband of a friend was entrusted with Caroline's business affairs and it appears that he proceeded systematically to rob the rather naïve Caroline while she devoted herself to writing poetry and reminiscences.

At some point her suspicions were aroused because she recorded that she had seen nothing of the proceeds of the sale of 29 Eversfield Place, which amounted to £1250. One by one all forty houses were sold, 'for which', she wrote, 'I never received a penny'.[15] Eventually her financial affairs were manipulated to such a degree that she was rendered bankrupt, to her complete bewilderment.

When she began to ask too many questions her 'friends' had her committed to lunatic asylums, twice at Haywards Heath and once in Camberwell, London. Details of her life after her release are at present unavailable, but it is know that she entered Hastings Union workhouse three times and eventually died there in 1889.

Historian Thomas Brett opined that she 'became demented and involved in pecuniary difficulties in consequence of her mania for hiring and letting of houses for which she was not adapted'; however, it seems likely that she was in fact cruelly swindled by those she trusted with her financial affairs.[16]

Mrs Terry:
Immovable object

Verbatim, from the *Hastings & St Leonards Observer* 16 March 1849.

"EJECTION EXTRAORDINARY

During yesterday, the inhabitants in the neighbourhood lying between Castle-street and Wellington-square were rendered spectators of a singular and somewhat unpleasant transaction connected with the attempted evictment of an aged female named Terry, who occupies an old house or rather cottage, near the corner of Castle-street.

Mrs. Terry's son, to whom the house belongs, is desirous of pulling down the old building and erecting a better, and accordingly has requested his mother to quit her ancient domicile and betake herself to another which he has prepared for her. Adopting the theory of the phrenologists, it appears that Mrs. Terry's organ of inhabitiveness is so largely developed, as to make her stoutly resist all entreaties or attempts made for her removal. Yesterday morning, the son proceeded to dismantle the maternal dwelling, which has lately been bolted and barred against all intruders by the jealous occupant.

The next step was to take the door off its hinges, and-the next to turn out the furniture, while the sashes were taken out.

Mrs. Terry made a desperate resistance to these proceedings, and although the house was stripped, resolutely maintained her post. At six o'clock last evening, she still remained in her dilapidated abode, and the police were obliged to be on the spot to prevent the collection of a mob."

A bright, sunny day in Hastings town centre 20 years after Mrs. Terry's sit-in. Taken from Robertson Street, the photo shows the Albert Memorial, constructed in 1863, and Wellington Place.

REFERENCES

[1] Including St Clement's, Halton, 1838; Fairlight, 1845; St Mary Magdalen, 1851; Holy Trinity 1857; Christ Church, Ore, 1858; St Matthew's, 1860; St John's, Hollington, 1865; St Helen's, Ore, 1869.

[2] Whitaker, B., 1974. *The Foundations: An Anatomy of Philanthropy and Society.* p. 48-50

[3] *Hastings & St Leonards Observer*, 13 February 1937, reminiscences from T. B. Brett, 1896.

[4] Brett, T. B., *Histories* Volume 2 p 169.

[5] A mere namesake of the Chief Engineer of the Metropolitan Board of Works, London.

[6] *Hastings & St Leonards News* 22 September 1865.

[7] He held the post for 40 years until his retirement in 1881 at the age of 79.

[8] This church was sold in about 1980 and now houses a Greek Orthodox congregation.

[9] Captain Mackay ruptured a blood vessel while dining with the Burtons at their house, Allegria, in 1834. Princess Victoria sent a messenger every day to enquire after his health.

[10] They won the 1st Coronation Prize in 1837, the Royal Victoria 1st prize in 1840, 1841, 1846 to 1849, and 1858; the 2nd Prize in 1844 and 1848; the gold bracelet from 1843 to 1847; the 2nd Prize in 1844, 1846 to 1848 and 1856; and the 1st Society's Prize in 1841 to 1844, and 1847.

[11] *Hastings & St Leonards News* 24 August 1849.

[12] The next day, Mrs. Barlow laid the first brick of St Leonards' Bo-Peep tunnel.

[13] Now called *The Uplands*.

[14] *Hastings & St Leonards News* 27 July 1861

[15] One of her homes was 2 Lorne Villas Silverhill.

[16] Brett, T. B. *Historico-Biographies* Volume II p.199. Some of Carey's poetry appears on pp 200-204.

CONCLUSION

The research which led to this book uncovered some data that I found surprising. The imbalance of the sexes in the western parishes was greater than I expected: in some areas two-thirds of the residents were female. This came about because wealthy widows and spinsters were attracted by the modern housing, space, clean air and social activities offered by the new town of St Leonards. The text of the 1861 anti-port Memorial suggests also that it was safe for women to go about unchaperoned, a freedom unheard of in certain other seaside towns, especially those with international harbours.

Equally surprising was the large number and the wide range of small businesses run by women. In an era when many areas of employment were closed to females, Hastings women seem to have infiltrated every possible alternative. Ironically, while they could not obtain work as accounts clerks, managers or book-keepers, women fulfilled all of these roles in their own businesses or that of their husbands. Women who would have been rejected had they applied for employment managing, for example, a decorating company or a brewery, ran such businesses with great success when as widows they took over their late husbands' affairs.

A brief look at the businesses run by women in the 1850s in Thanet, a comparable southern seaside area in nearby Kent, revealed that Hastings had far more women in business, especially in the areas of food retailing and beer-shop keeping. It is likely that Hastings' fishing industry is partly responsible: the fluctuations in fishermen's earnings and the danger inherent in the job perhaps led more wives to seek an income of their own. The number of milliners and dressmakers in an area is related to the number of women residents, and to their wealth, so it comes as no surprise that Hastings had many more than Thanet. Mid-Victorian women in business in Thanet with no counterpart in Hastings included an estate and insurance agent, a livery stable keeper, a photographer, a jeweller, an optician, a stonemason and two oyster dealers.

Professionally, Hastings women had many similarities with women in other parts of England; the main difference was the lack of any major industry, such as textile mills for example, which employed large numbers of women. This impacted on women's involvement with the rudimentary trade union movement. However, Hastings washerwomen went on strike and won their case, despite working for a variety of employers.

The large number of prostitutes is, perhaps, not something one would expect in so small a town, particularly one without an international port, and where the female sex predominated. It is undoubtedly a result of the terrible poverty in the Old Town and at Halton, where these 'unfortunates' were based. It was partly owing to the large number operating in Hastings that ladies signed the aforementioned anti-harbour Memorial. Sailors on shore-leave would have attracted greater numbers of prostitutes to the town and encouraged even more local women to turn to the streets for a living. Another surprise was the sheer brazenness of these women, some of whom even seemed proud of their occupation. They proved ready and able to defend themselves and their associates - verbally and physically - at a moment's notice, and were highly visible and audible around the town, soliciting in the streets, drinking in pubs and beer-shops, and fighting and arguing amongst themselves.

Although modern-day secondary sources have to some extent exploded the myth of passive and docile Victorian womanhood, my research revealed an unexpectedly large amount of drunkenness and violence by, and among, working-class women. The most surprising finding of this research was the number of homicides committed by women: two murdered their husbands, one of whom also killed two of her sons, and dozens committed infanticide. Over the same research period (1848-1870) I failed to find a single newspaper report of a local man killing his wife or child.

In the early to mid-Victorian era, women were supposedly confined to the domestic sphere, but women in Hastings were very much in the public eye. When visitors arrived they were often greeted by a female lodging house keeper and everywhere they went they saw women working as shop-keepers, shop assistants, milliners and dressmakers. Hastings' most popular tourist-attractions - the Caves, the Castle, the bathing machines and the warm baths, all had female proprietors and staff, and religious establishments employed women pew-openers and chapel-keepers. Women street-beggars and street-sellers abounded, female fish-hawkers pushed their barrows along the roads of the Old Town. Female servants ran errands, swept paths, scrubbed front steps and polished windows. In hotels, women were waitresses, chambermaids, barmaids and proprietors and they served in pubs and beer-shops, while others visited, as customers and as vendors of sea food and chestnuts. Laundresses were seen spreading out linen to dry on the beaches and hillsides. In the gaol, workhouse and infirmary, women were matrons and nurses. Local newspapers advertised women tutors of singing, dancing and music and female-run seminaries and schools. In the theatres, women acted, sung and danced, and they were among the circus-performers. Women rode around town on horseback and in open carriages, and thronged the shopping streets and arcades. And women filled the churches to such an extent that male worshippers could hardly find pew-space anywhere in either town.

It is unfortunate that more could not have been included about domestic life. However, research is reliant on surviving documentation, and the only matters documented were either official or out-of-the-ordinary. Information on women's work is, therefore, far easier to come by than data on domestic life. There is, however, no reason to suppose that home life in Hastings was any different to that in other parts of England, and information on domestic life is widely available from a range of other social history sources and works of Victorian fiction. My forthcoming book *Down & Out in Victorian Hastings* will, hopefully, at least be able to describe domestic life among the impoverished.

APPENDICES
Women's work in Hastings & St Leonards 1800-1872

Note: The bracketed dates in these appendices have the following meanings. Single dates refer to the source and dates separated by a dash denote the length of tenure.
     Mrs J Smith, 11 Colonnade (1839)
     Jemima Bailey, 6 The Bourne (186-57)
-Data from three sources of different dates are shown thus -
     Ann Jones, 55 Marina (1839; 1851;1852)
We cannot tell when Ann arrived, nor when she left, only that she was recorded there at these dates. It is only an assumption that she was there continuously.

FEMALE LICENSEES OF HOTELS AND PUBLIC HOUSES 1800-1872.

This list is incomplete because there is no central record of licensees. It was gleaned from many sources including license applications, trade directories, court reports, Censuses and secondary sources.

1800 –1840

The Swan, High Street. Henrietta Collier (on death of her father John, 5 times Mayor).
The Bull, Bulverhythe. Mrs. Hannah Davis (granted license April 1826).
The Bull, Bulverhythe, Elizabeth Wilkinson (1833-34).
The Hastings Arms, George Street. Ann Sargent (1821-1824).[1]
Royal Oak, Castle Street. Ann Sargent (1825-29).[2]
The Cinque Port Arms, All Saints' Street. Judith Wood (1828-30).
The Anchor, 13 George Street. Ann Thwaites. (1800-1804).
The Cutter, 12 East Parade, Mrs. Elizabeth Bell (1823-1836).
The Crown, Courthouse Street. Sarah Smith (1815-1831)
Jolly Fisherman, East Street. Mrs. James Mann.
The Crown, Courthouse Street. Sarah Smith. (1815-1832).
The George, 120 All Saints' Street. Rebecca Furby (1833-35).

1840s to 1860s

Warrior's Gate Norman Road West, Catherine Pilcher. Innkeeper (1841).
The Norman Hotel, Norman Road East. Elizabeth Benton Young (1853).
The Bull, Bulverhythe. Miss Sheather (until 1852).
The Swan, High Street. Elizabeth Carswell (1858-1873).
*The Castle Hotel & Posting House,*Wellington Square. Frances Emary (1854-55 & 1862).
Priory Family Hotel, 24 Robertson Street. Mary Ann & Ellen Eldridge (1851 & 54).

Marina Inn, 3 Sussex Road. Mrs. Helen Bennett (1862).

The George, 120 All Saints' Street. Mrs. Rebecca Wood (1852 & 1854; until 1861).

Railway & Commercial Hotel, 20 Havelock Road. Mary Ann Eldridge (1854 & 55).

The Bricklayer's Arms, Bohemia Terrace. Miss Young (1853).

The Albert, 17-18 Undercliffe. Mrs. Ann Hutchings.

The Anchor, Mews Road, East Ascent. Miss Mary Ballard (1852).

The Wheatsheaf Inn, Spittleman Down (Bohemia Terr). Mrs. Sarah Gorring (1848-1852).

The Angel, St Mary's Terrace. Miss Barbara Ticehurst (1852).

Halton Tavern. Elizabeth Goodwin (1863).

The Angel, St Mary's Terrace. Mrs. Lucy Scott (1864 – died 1866).

Jolly Fisherman, East Street. Mrs. Swaine (1864).

The Prince Albert, Rock-a-Nore Road. Mrs. Rachel Pomphrey (1862; until 1865).

The Jenny Lind, High Street. Mary Robinson (1866)(until 1870).

The Royal Oak, Castle St. Mrs. Ann Yates (June to September 1864).

The Lion Inn, Stone Street. Ann Bean (1865 - 1866).

The Britannia, Bourne Street. Harriett Vinall (1866).

The George, 120 All Saints' Street. Sarah C. Gorley (1867&169).

Duke of York, 5 Union Road, St Leonards. Mrs. Hill (1867).

The Albion Hotel, Marine Parade. Harriet Bowles (1866).

The Albion Hotel, Marine Parade. Mrs. Ellis (1869).

The Cutter, 12 East Parade. Mrs. Harriet Dunk.

Provincial Hotel, 18 Havelock Road. Mrs Montague (1869).

York Hotel, (?) 17 York Buildings. Mrs. Osborne (until 1870).

The Dun Cow (or Horse), Albion Terrace, Halton. Mrs. Jane Cox (1867-).

1870-1872

Provincial Hotel, 18 Havelock Road. Miss Mary Ann Montague (1871).

Commercial Hotel and Dining Rooms. Mrs. Linney (1871).

Duke of York, 5 Union Road, St Leonards. Mrs. Mary Fairhall (1871).

The Albion Hotel, Marine Parade. Susan Emary.

The Hare and Hounds Inn, Ore. Frances Tritton.[3]

The Crown Inn, Courthouse Street. Mrs. Catherine Stride (1872).

Green's Family and Commercial Hotel, Havelock Rd. Mrs. Eliza Green.

The Hastings Arms, 2 George Street. Mary Ann Ray, (1870-1871).

The Cricketers Arms, Waldegrave Street. Mary Ann Mitchell (until 1870).

The Norman Hotel, Norman Road East. Mrs. Elizabeth Palmer.

The Stag Inn, 15 All Saints' Street. Mrs. P. Jenkins (1871).

The Stag Inn, 15 All Saints' Street. Mrs. Mary Heathfield (1872) (Also the freeholder).

St Leonards Arms, 6 London Road/Shepherd Street. Miss Mary Semark (1872).

Prince of Wales, 9 Melbourne Terrace, Bohemia. Harriet Hayden (1872).

Harrow Inn, Hollington. Mary Robertson.

Bo-peep Inn, Elizabeth Payne. (1871) (Also the freeholder).

Duke of Cornwall, Post Office Passage. Charlotte Wenham (jointly with husband).

White Lion, 7 St Michael's Terrace. Miss Harriet Perigoe.

The New Ship, West Street. Frances Hope (lost license 1874).

The Globe, Meadow Road. Harriet Turner (1872).

Plasterers Arms, South Street. Mary Ann Ranger (1872).

Coach & Horses, East Ascent. Jane Taylor (1872). (Also the freeholder.)

Lord Nelson, Bourne Street. Charlotte Clarke (1872).

The Tiger, 13 Stonefield Road. Mrs. Philly Jenkins.

Brewery Taps, licensed victuallers and beer shops 1840-1871.

The Castle Brewery Tap. Mrs. Paine.
The Castle Brewery Tap, 11 Wellington Terrace. Harriet Cheale (1869) & 1872).
The Swan Tap, High St. Miss Mary Rosina Willett (1861).
The Sussex Tap. Mrs. Jemima French.
Fisher's Refreshment Bar, High Street. Mrs. Fisher (1871).
Refreshment bar, 50 George Street. Miss Lock (1864).
Diamond Inn Beer Shop, Bourne Walk. Elizabeth Pomphrey Sargeant (1864).
The Black Horse Beer Shop, Shepherd Street. Harriet Stephenson (1864).
The Dun Cow (or Horse), Albion Terrace, Halton. Mrs. Jane Cox. (1863-1867).[4]
New Inn Beerhouse, Market Place. Miss Frances Burton.
The Privateer, Wellington Mews. Mrs. Ellen Brazier (until 1852).
Alma Beer Shop, All Saints' Street. Mrs. Ann Tyril (Tyrell?) (jointly with husband).
Albert Inn Beer-shop, 33 North Street. Elizabeth Cull (1861).
The Forester's Arms Beer-house, 6 East Parade. Frances Hope.
Fisherman's Home, 6 East Hill Passage. Ellen Lester (1872).
The Railway, Gensing Station Road. Mary Campbell (1872).
The Old House at Home Beer-house, 44 All Saints Street. Elizabeth Cull.
Talbot House beer-shop, 16 Lennox St, Halton. Ann Friend, licensed victualler.
The Mackeral beer-shop. Mrs. Huggett (1856).
The Bricklayer's Arms, Bohemia Terrace. Fanny Jenks (Jinks?) (1865).
Beer-shop, West Beach Street. Mrs. Jane Piper.
Beer-shop, 25 Bourne Street. Mrs. Maria Elphick
Beer-shop, 4 Hill Street. Mary Glyde.
Beer-shop, East Beach Street. Ann Tassell.
Beer-shop, 2 Stonefield Road. Charlotte Bourne.
Beer-seller, 1 Waterloo Place. Lucy Scott (1851).
Licensed victualler, 3 Sussex Place. Helen Bennett (1865 & 1867).
Beer retailer, 32 West Street. Frances Hope (1861).
Beer retailer, 30 West Street. Mrs. Frances Burton.
Beer retailer, West Beach Street. Mrs. Jane Piper.
Beer-shop keeper, 9 Lavatoria. Caroline Barnes.
Beer-house, 6 St Mary's Terrace. Jane Pilcher (1872).
Beer-shop, 1-2 Dorset Place. Elizabeth Collins (1871) (Also the freeholder).
Beer-shop, 8 Dorset Place. Mrs. Jane Rose.
Beer-shop, Wellington Court. Martha Card. (1873).

Female owners of public houses and beer shops, 1872.

Public house owners
Kate and Frances Burfield (11 owned).
Elizabeth Ridley.
Mary Heathfield.
Harriet Fisher.
Mary Creasy Vickery.
Ann Yates (lived in London, owned the *Royal Oak*).
Charlotte Mann.
Mary Reeves.
Mary Ann Adgo.

Beer shop owners
Mrs. Jane Harvey – Eagle, Bourne St.
Mary Dowsett – Market Tavern.
Mary Heathfield.
Kate & Frances Burfield (owned three, including the *British Queen,* North Street).
Harriet Cheale (also licensee).
Frances Kingsnorth – 8 Castle Terrace.
Eliza Lord – 32 West Street.
Mary Ann Dowsett – 14 Hill Street.
Eliza Collins (also licensee).
Ann How – *Prince of Wales*, 9 Melbourne Place.

BUSINESSES 1817-1862

This list includes only women who were listed as proprietors in their own right. It is not exhaustive. Records are missing that would have provided a good many more names. Please note that lodging-house and boarding-house keepers have been omitted, as there were far too many of them to include. The sources are Brett's manuscript history, Censuses 1841, 1851 and 1861; Powell's Directory 1817; Pigot's Directory 1839; Kelly's Directory 1845 and 1852; Home Counties Directory 1851; Osborne's Directory 1852, 1857 and 1858 and Sussex Directory 1855 and 1859.

All trades 1821-1839

Confectioner, Mrs. Stone, 45 High Street.
Dressmaker, Miss Evershed (1821).
Fancy repository, Eliza Gardner, 28 George St.
Fancy repository, 'by the new Warm Baths', Mrs. Roe. (1824) Later 1 East Parade.
Fruiterer, Charlotte Osborne, Mrs. 55 George Street (1826-28).
Fruiterer, Elizabeth Ball, George Street.
Greengrocer, Mrs. J. Phillips (also let lodgings) (1817).
Laundress, Fanny Gower, Back Street (1831).
Laundry proprietor, Mrs. Ann Tapp. (c1834-54).
Milliners:

        Catherine Fox, 34 High Street (1832-4).
        Charlotte Greatrex (1832-34).
        Sarah Poile (1832-4).
        Mary Ross, Pelham Place (1832-4).
        Frances Tooth, 1 Castle Street (1832-4).
        Elizabeth Whitfield 46 George Street (1832-4).
        Keziah Allen, Hill Street (1824).
        Elizabeth Ellis, High Street (1824).
        Ann Evershed, West Street (1832-4).
        Susannah Hambrey, High Street (1824).
        Ann Reynolds, 12 High Street (1832-4).
        May Ellis, 6 George Street (1826-28).
        Mrs. Fisher, 84 High Street (1826-28).
        Sarah Soane, 6 Castle Street (1831).

Mrs Bailey, 5 Dorset Place.

Mrs Barker, Lower Trinity Terrace.

Mrs Broadhurst, 12 Norman Rd West.

Miss Gibbons, 26 London Rd.

Poulterer, Ann Adams 66 High Street (1824-32).

Repository, Mrs. Elizabeth Cohen, 2 Pelham Place (1826-28).

Tea dealer, Miss Eaton (1831).

Seedsman & florist, Sarah Walker, 6 Gensing Road.

Shopkeeper, Mary Brazier, Bourne Street (1824).

Stationer, Sarah Smith, 22 George Street.

Straw hat makers (1824-32):

Jane Carr, 45 George Street.

Eliza Fox, 34 High Street.

Hannah Hull, East Street.

Susannah Hambrey, High Street (1824).

Rachel Sargeant, 3 Castle Street (1824-28).

Ann Garlick, All Saints' Street (1824).

Hannah Ives, John Street (1824).

FEMALE RETAILERS 1839-1861

Miscellaneous non-provision shops 1839-1861

Baby linen dealer and child's dressmaker, Emma Palmer, 25 Castle Street.

Baby linen dealer, Janet Miller, 25 Castle Street (1845;1859).

Berlin wool repositories:

Mrs. Charlotte Osborne, 55 George Street.

Louisa Soane. 10 Bedford place (1859). Later 119 All Saints' Street.

Amelia Burt, Central Arcade.

Mrs Day, 36 Robertson St.

Mrs Phoebe Ellis, 2 Church St.

Books and stationery, etc:

Bookseller, Sarah Austin, Marine Parade (1824).

Bookseller, Eleanor Slade, 16½ High Street (1839 & 1840).

Bookseller, Mary Tilley, High Street (1841).

Fancy stationer, Victoria Weston, 60 High Street (1859).

Library & stationer, Ann Holt, 24 White Rock (1838- 1872).[5]

Brokers:

Jane Hadden, 93 All Saints' Street.

Elizabeth Boulter, 21 John Street.

Elizabeth Baker, Winding Lane (1841).

China & glass dealers:

Mrs. Groves, 36 Norman Road West.

Mrs. Hastelow, 25 Norman Road West (1867).

Mrs. Hannah Morton,. 26-7 (later 43) High Street, 13 Castle St, 72 Norman Rd.

Clothes dealers (secondhand):

Wardrobe dealer, Mrs. Elizabeth Snashall, 2 Bourne Street (later 1 Union St).

Clothier, Mrs. Bell, 57 All Saints' Street.

Clothes dealer, Sophia Penney, All Saints' Street (1866).

Coal merchant, Eliza Ann Deudney, 43 (later 104) Marina.

Corn chandler, Mary Crippen, High Street (1841).

Earthenware dealer, Hannah Green, cottage near the Hare & Hounds, Ore.

Fancy shops:

       Miss Sandy, 37 Marina.

       Mrs J Smith, 13 Colonnade (1839).

       Miss Standen, 25 East Ascent.

       Elizabeth Cohen, 10 Castle Street.

       Mrs. Wood, 37 George Street.

       Ann Reynolds, 37 Marina (1839; 1841; 1851;1852).

       Charlotte Weston, 60 High Street (1861).

       Mrs. Day, 26 Robertson Street.

Furniture broker, Elizabeth Baker, Mrs. 26 High Street.

Ironmongers:

       Sarah Offen, Mrs, 3 Norman Road West.

       Charlotte Mann, 7 East Ascent.

Ladies' outfitters:

       Mrs. Hall, 32 London Road.

       & milliner, Mary Hardcastle, 33 Robertson Street (1867).

       Elizabeth Northey, 30 Robertson Street (1862).

       & milliner, Emily Hunter, 23 Robertson Street (1862 & 1867).

       Mrs. Phillips, 6 Central Arcade (1861).

Linen drapers:

       Charlotte Green, 28 George Street (1839).

       Mrs. Hampton, 25 George Street.

       Mrs. Harriet Bell, 36 (later 57) All Saints' Street.

       Mrs. Philpott, 38 Marina.

       Miss Miller, 25 Castle Street (from 1852).

Perfumier, Miss Bollin, Wellington Place (1857).

Second hand clothes dealers:

       Mrs. Stone, North Street.

       Ann Pomphrey, 7 Bourne Passage (1861).

       Miss Walder, 60 All Saints' Street (died 1860).

       Mrs. Hall, 7 Gensing Station Road (1867).

Shell Artiste, Sarah Ranger, 5 Wellington Terrace.

Shell worker, Mary Ann Hide, Pleasant Row.

Shell dealer, (British & Foreign) Mrs. Elizabeth Oliver, Marine Parade, later 34 West St.

Shell dealer, Susan Philcox, 7 Denmark Place.

Shell dealer, Sarah Hide, 3 Pleasant Row.

Stationer, Sarah Bryant, 84 High Street (1839).

Stationer, Charlotte Osborne, Mrs. 27 Castle Street.

Stationer & straw bonnet maker, Mrs. Smith, 13 South Colonnade (Marina).

Stationer & tea dealer, Mrs. Mary Cope, 115 Marina.

Tea and fancy dealer, Mrs. Elizabeth Pitter, 7 George Street.

Tea dealer, Sophia Abbott, 33 West Street (1839).

Tallow Chandler, Alice Guedella, 6 Castle Hill. (1861).

Tobacconists:

       Harriet Bate, 26 Castle Street.

       Mrs. Anna Barker, 47 Robertson Street.

Toy dealers:

       Mrs. Charlotte Wood, 37 George Street.

       Mrs J.B. Funnell, Central Arcade.

       Mary Roe, Marine Parade (1824-28 & 1839), Fishmarket (1832).

       Charlotte Playden, 130 All Saints' Street.

Watch-mender and maker, Charlotte Weston, Mrs. 60 High Street (1859).

Miscellaneous provision shops 1839-1861)

Apple shop keeper, Elizabeth Phillips, 14 John Street (1861).
Bakers:

      Mrs. Felstead, 5 Castle Road.

      Mrs. Shackleford, bread and biscuit dealer, 5 Castle Road.

      Mrs. Harriot Beck, 4 London Road (1851&1861). Also corn merchant.

      Mrs. Rosina Vine, Mercatoria (1861).

      Mrs. Harriet Ranger, 16 Stone Street (1854).

      Mrs. Jane Smith, 56 High Street (1854).

      Sarah Betts, 26 Bourne Street.

      Maria Pitt, 5 Bank Buildings.

      Mrs. Elizabeth Elphick, 43 Norman Road West.

Confectioners:

      Elizabeth Ball, 2 Castle Terrace.

      Eliza Newberry, 7 George Street (1861).

      Mrs. G. Wheeler, 17-18 High Street.

      Sarah Ballard, 17 Castle Street (1871).

      Confectioner & fruiterer, Mrs. Charlotte Wheeler, 17 High Street.

      Confectioner & fruiterer, Sarah & John Wheeler, 17 High Street.

Cowkeepers:

      Mrs Frances Whiteman,. 6 Courthouse Street.

      Mrs. Mary Maria Standen, 15 Stone Street.

Dairywoman, Elizabeth Stevens, Bohemia Farm.

Egg merchant & Poulterer, Madame Sophia Flouré, 61½ George Street.

Farmer, Mrs. Elizabeth Foster, Priory Farm.

Fish sellers and fishmongers:

      Mary Ann Foster, Tamarisk Steps.

      Kitty White, Waterloo Passage.

      Sarah Marten, 64 All Saints' Street.

      Sarah Mause, 64 All Saints' Street (1851).

      Sarah Taught, Hoppers Passage.

      Harriot Craig, 2 Creek.

      Ann Mann, 3 Creek. (1861).

      Sarah Mann, Williams Row (1851).

      Naomi Master, 3 Creek. (1861).

      Emma Willis, Bourne Street (1861).

      Ann. Noakes.

      Margaret Tassell, East Street.

Fruiterers:

      Ann Guy, 60 George Street (1839).

      Mrs.Harriet Marsh, (1861).

      Fruiterer/grocer, Mrs. Burt, Market Passage.

      Fruiterer and greengrocer, Mrs. Mary Ann Taylor, 61 George Street.

      Fruiterer & greengrocer, Mrs. Mahala Standen, 6 Castle Road.

      Fruiterer & greengrocer, Mrs. Ann Walter, 6 South Colonnade (1851).

      Fruiterer & seed dealer & greengrocer, Mrs.Ann Golding, 20 Hill Street, later
      16 George Street, 18 &19 George St, 42½ High Street.

Greengrocers:

      Mrs. Harriet Hyder, Norman Road West (1859).

      Sarah Richardson, 47 All Saints' Street.

      Ann Mills, 10 Prospect Place.

      Mary Kennard, 135 All Saints' Street.

Charlotte Hinkley, 124 All Saints' Street.

Eliza Paris, 103 All Saints' Street.

Elizabeth Fulmer, 22 Shepherd Street.

Harriot Cramp 128 All Saints' Street ('pauper-greengrocer').

Mary Ann Ranger, Mrs. 37 London Road.

Maria Baker, High Street (1841).

Mary Philpot, Market Passage.

Mary Kent, East Bourne Street (1861).

Sarah Pomphrey, 21 High Street.

Winifred Burt, 10 West Street.

Mary Hadden, 118 All Saints' Street.

Mary Harris, 31 High Street. (Married to a butcher) (1861).

Mary Bailey, Market. (1867).

Greengrocer & Beerseller, Lucy Scott, 1 Waterloo Place.

Grocers:

Mary Stewart, Courthouse Street (1841).

Mrs. May (no address).

Ann Reeves, Courthouse Street (1841).

Mrs. Oaks, East Parade. (1854).

Elizabeth Blackman, Halton Fields (1839).

Mary Monday, 6 Stone Street (1839).

Sarah Jones, Barrack Ground (1839).

Mary Ann Stewart, 50 High Street.

Ann Palk, Wellington Court (1839).

Mrs Baker, 4 St Andrew's Terrace.

Mrs Blayden, 129 Al Saints' Street.

Mrs Filmer, Shepherd Street.

Jane Smith, 104 All Saints' Street (1861).

Charlotte Blayden, 129 All Saints' Street.

Eliza Guess, 2 Hill Street.

Mrs. Margaret White, Bourne Street; later 1, Pleasant Row.

Elizabeth White, Bourne Street (1861).

Mrs. Mary Ann Ranger, 3 Mercatoria.[6]

Sarah Jones, 33 Bohemia Terrace.

Mary Ann Hewert, 50 All Saints Street.

Sarah White, 75 All Saints' Street.

Susannah Betts, 103 All Saints' Street. [7]

Theodosia Baker, 4 High Street.

Mary Ann Welfare, 137 All Saints' Street (1861).[8]

Elizabeth Bray, Sussex Road. (1867).

Ann Maria Lock, 50 (later 51) George Street(1867).

Grocer, newsagent, tobacconist, Eliza and Jane Smith, 31 High Street.

Milk Vendor, Elizabeth Smale, 1 Providence Row.

Pork butcher, Mrs. Whiteman, Courthouse Street.(1854).

Poulterers (licensed):

Mrs. Ann Stace, 2 Castle Street (1867- died 1872).

Mrs. Polhill, 4 Robertson Street (1857).

Mrs. Ann Roberts, Market Place (1862).

Shopkeepers:

Mrs. Ann Bishop, Gensing Road.

Mrs.Ann Cousins, Hill Street.

Mrs. Ann Mills, 5 Claremont.

Ann News, 8 All Saints' Street (1861).

Mary Larkin, 22 All Saints' Street (1861).

Mrs. Elizabeth Stoakes, 64 All Saints' Street.

Mrs. Mary White, 102 All Saints' Street.

Ann Bailey, 29 Bourne Street. (1861) (stallholder, Hastings Market).

Elizabeth Jones, 131 All Saints' Street (1867).

Mrs. Theodosia Baker, St Andrews Terrace.

Mrs. Jane Knott, Cuckoo Hill.

Mrs. Ann New, 8 All Saints' Street.

Mrs. Matilda Catt, Bohemia Terrace (jointly with husband).

Mrs. Harriet Ranger, 67 St Mary's Terrace.

Eliza Kent. 58 All Saints' Street.

Mrs.Ann Gallopp, 6 St Mary's Terrace.

Mary Boreham, 10 Hill Street (1861).

Jane Brazier, South Eastern Cottage, next to 9 Wellington Mews.

Jane Connor, 20 High Street (1867).

Mrs. A. Button, West Street. (1867).

Street sellers:

Shrimp hawker, Sarah Martin, 112 All Saints' St.[9]

Huckster (hawker), Elizabeth, Isabella & Matilda Prior, 3 Fountain Road.

Flowergirl. Sarah Offon, hut behind 94 All Saints' Street, age 12.

Hawker, Lucy Lewer, Ore Down.

Licensed hawker, Mary Curteiss, 3 West Street.

Wine merchant, (retired) Mary Ann Wells, 12 High Street (1861).

FEMALE MANUFACTURERS 1839-1861

Boot and shoe maker, Mrs. Mary Sadler, 25 Norman Road West.

Boot closer, Mahala Kingham, behind Bourne Street.

Boot and shoe binders:

Lois Jarrett, 4 Zion Cottages.

Harriet Martin, London Road.

Mary Ann Godden, 143 All Saints' Street.

Frances Elphick, 4 Mount Pleasant.

Ann Robertson, 112 All Saints' Street.

Ellen Barker, 24 Stonefield Road.

Martha Gallop, 23 Stonefield Road.

Jemima Woodgate, 5 Russell Street.

Frances Boreham, 5 Waterloo Place (1861).

Elizabeth Carey, 5 Waterloo Place (1861).

Frances Carey, 5 East Hill Passage (1851).

Sarah Sherwood, 5 Waterloo Place (1861).

Elizabeth Brazier, 11 West Hill Cottages.

Elizabeth Hanson, 5 Caves Road.

Eliza Williams, behind 24 Bourne Street (1861).

Sarah Searwood, 5 East Hill Passage.

Catherine Goodwin, 1 Strong Passage.

Emma Haines, 64 All Saints' Street.

Ellen Turner, 44 All Saints' Street.

Sarah Wood, 18 All Saints' Street.

Bonnetmaker, Ellen Wheeler, 17 George Street. (1861).

Dressmakers: far too numerous to list.

Dressmaker - milliners:

Emily Bourner, North Terrace, Halton.

Catherine Griffin, Mrs. 54 (later 55) All Saints' Street.

Emily and Harriet Barrow, 6 Castle Terrace.

Mme Victorine Winsor, 4 Stratford Place.[10]

Embroiderer, Ann Graves, 2 Castle Hill (1861).

Furrier and feather dresser, Mrs. Clarissa Hargrave, 6 Waterloo Place (1851).

Furrier & leather dresser, Mrs. Jemima Johnson, 72½ High Street (1839).

French paper flower maker, Jane Gill, 9 High Street.[11]

Hatters:

Mrs. Ann Lott, 58 George Street (1852 & 1855).[12]

Harriet Breeds, 58 George Street (1859).

Hosier, (also glovier, shirtmaker). Mrs Undine Pegge, 31 Robertson Street.

Lace manufacturer, Martha Healey, 20 Castle Street (1851).

Lacemakers:

Elizabeth Hope, Wyatt's Cottages, Ore.

Sarah Rottedge, Wyatt's Cottages, Ore.

Lace runner, Rebecca Stead, 7 St Thomas' Cottages.

Mantlemakers:

Elizabeth Patching, 27 High Street.

Beney & Mallyon, Misses, 2 Castle Place.

Milliners:

Ann Bridges, Wellington Mews (1841).

Naomi Cowper, St Andrews Terrace (1841).

Caroline Shaw, Norman Road West (1841).

Mrs. Skinner, 46 George Street. (opened April 1859).

Drapery, hosiery, lace and millinery. Eliza Bailey, Mrs, Cuckoo Hill.

Mrs. Day, 31 High Street.

Caroline Fermor, 22 George Street.

Mrs. E. Fisher, 101 All Saints' Street.

Mrs. Esther Baily, 18 Robertson Street (Also mantle maker).

Mary Vine, 2 Mercatoria.

Sarah Pomphrey, 3 West Street.

Emily Pierce, 35 High Street.

Louisa Smith, 17 Stone Street.

Mary Ann Smith, Mrs. 20 Castle Street (1855).

Louisa Smith, 31 St Andrew's Terrace (1851).

Mary Watson, 8 Russell Street.

Mrs. Leak, 1 West Street (1867).

Mrs. Hutchinson, 7 Western Road (1867).

Mrs. Chandler, 5 Stone Street (1867).

Mrs. H Hughes, 5 Mercatoria (1867).

Mrs. Johnson, 15 George Street (1867).

Mrs. Barker, Lower Trinity Terrace (1867).

Mrs. Brett, 7 Mercatoria (1867).

Mrs. Bailey, 5 Dorset Place (1867).

Miss Palmer, 25 Castle Street (to 1852).

Mrs. Ann Peckham, 2 High Street (1859).

Milliner & dressmakers:

Mrs. Caroline Harris, 39½ High Street.

Mrs. Louisa Honiss, 5 York Place.

Mrs. Frances Tooth, 4 Castle Street.

Mrs. Anne Edwards, Cavendish Cottage.

Mrs. Catherine Tapp, 3 Burdett Place, George Street.

Mrs. Mary Ann Taylor, Pleasant Row.

Mrs. Elizabeth Row, 3 South Terrace, Halton.

Milliner & Juvenile warehouse[13], Mrs. Charlotte McArthur, 1 Sea View Cottage.

Milliner & Berlin wool warehouse, Mrs. Louisa Soane, 59 High Street (1851).

Milliner, Juvenile warehouse & ladies' outfitter, Mrs. Mary Ann Lye, 25 George Street.

Milliner & Cloak maker, Mrs. Esther Bailey, 18 Robertson Street.

Milliner, stay & crinoline warehouse, dressmaker and fancy toy shop. Mrs. Pears, 45 Robertson Street (1864).[14]

Needlewomen, seamstresses and sempstresses:

      Mary Taylor, North Street (1841).

      Sarah Deeprose, London Road (1841).

      Mary Tulley, Mercatoria.

      Lucy Beddoes, Wingfield Cottage.

      Harriet Foster, 28 All Saints' Street.

      Charlotte Breach, 69 All Saints' Street.

      Ann Seagrave, 6 Stone Street.

      Ann Harman, 114 All Saints' Street.

      The Misses Philpot, 37 Marina (since 1830s).

Stay and corsetmakers:

      Sarah Daniell, 89 High Street (1839).

      Sarah Poile, 45 (later 61½) George Street (1839).

      Ann Russell, 6 Pelham Arcade (1839).

      Mary Ann Fullager, 33 Robertson Street (1839).

      Sophia and Ann Goldsmith, 7 Waterloo Place (1850s).

      Sophia Goldsmith, 3 Waterloo Place (1861).

      Mrs. Pace, Brook Estate. Later 65 George Street.

      Sarah Daniels, Mrs. & Mary Jeffrey, Mrs. 36 High Street (1850s).

      Jane Wallis, 109 All Saints' Street.

      Mary Ann Fullager, 33 Robertson Street.

      Mrs. Elizabeth Pollard, 65 St Mary's Terrace.

      Mrs. A Honiss, 5 York Place (Stay Warehouse).

      Hannah Phillips, 7 Barley Lane.

      (& trimming seller) Mrs. Louisa Bolingbroke, 48 Robertson Street.

      Misses MA and ME Greenaway, 16 Wellington Place (1867).

Tailoresses:

      Eliza Parkes, 71 High Street.

      Ann Broadbridge, 1 Coborg Place (1861).

      Hannah French, North Row, Ore

Upholsteresses:

      Charlotte Morley, 5 Market Terrace.

      Emmeline Morley. 5 Market Terrace (daughter of the above).

      Ann & Elizabeth Grady, Tackleway (1851).

      Ann & Elizabeth Grady, 6 Vine's Row (1861).

      Mrs Walker, 1 Meadow Cottage.

      Elizabeth Marrell, 2 Wood's Row.

      Eliza Hemmings, 9 St Michael's Cottages, Stonefield Street.

Straw bonnet and hat manufacturers:

      Elizabeth Smith, Norman Road East (1841).

      Mary Smith, Norman Road East (1841).

      Elizabeth Hough, Norman Road West (1841).

      Miss Pearce, 35 High Street.

      Charlotte Harmer, 2 St Michael's Terrace.

      Mrs. Payne, George Street (1839).

      Mrs. Louisa Pollard, Courthouse Street (1839;1851).[15]

Mrs. Louisa and Miss Jane Pollard, 102 High Street (1859).
Louisa Pollard, 104 High Street (1861).
Mrs. Ann Lansdell, 3 Bentinck Cottage.
Harriet Walker, 1 Meadow Cottage (1851).
Harriet and Mary Ann Walker, 1 Meadow Cottage (1859).
Ann Walker, 3 Waterloo Place.
Sophia Goldsmith, 3 Waterloo Place (1861).
Miss Walker, 122 All Saints' Street.
Mrs. Judith Carpenter, 104 High Street (also let lodgings).
Mrs. Jane Carr, 45½ George Street (also let lodgings) (1817).
Mrs. Hide, All Saints' Street.
Mrs. Elizabeth Foord, 22 Bourne Street, later 61 George Street.
Miss Pierce, 35 High Street.
Emily Pierce, 67 High Street (also milliner).
Mrs. Hannah Ives, 18 (later 44) George Street.
Jane Phillips, Parade.
Mary Ann Glazier, Amphion Place, later 69 All Saints' Street.
Emily Hill, 2 Waterloo Place.
Miss Slough, Norman Road West.
Ellen Trotter, 1 Gensing Road.
Ann Humphreys, Hastings Cottage.
Mrs. Holder, 89 High Street (1867).

Silk worker, Eliza Foster, Derby Arms, 1 Union Rd.
Silk weavers:

(formerly) Elizabeth Hope, Wyatt's Cottages.
Elizabeth Turner, London Road, Ore.
Harriet Pritchard, 7 Pleasant Row (1861).

WOMEN IN SERVICE INDUSTRIES 1817-1861

Bathing machine proprietors:

Mrs. Cobby, Parade (1848).
Mrs. Lois Picknell. Victoria Cottage, Kentish Place.
Mrs White.
Maria Robinson, 32 St Andrew's Terrace.

Bathing establishments:

Manager, Pelham Baths (1851): Mrs. Martha Thatcher (b1792 - d1857).[16]
Proprietor, Pelham Baths (1857): Miss Ellen Thatcher.
Managers of St Leonards Baths: Mr. & Mrs. Barnes.
Manager, Hastings Old Baths: Mrs. Neal.
Attendant of Royal Baths, Marina: Mrs. Roberts.
Proprietresses of Pelham Baths: Mrs. and the Misses Emary (1870).
Proprietress, Royal Baths (opposite Victoria Hòtel). Mrs. Parker (1870).

Blacksmith & Shoeing, Mrs. M. Ranger. West Street & 14 Shepherd St.
Cabinet maker, upholsterer and undertaker, Sarah Eldridge, Mrs. 34½ High Street.
Carriers of luggage and goods:

Mrs. B Quaife, 4 Alfred Street (1871).
Carrier to Ore: Mrs. Crump, Breed's Yard (1867).
Carrier to Bexhill: Elizabeth Gander (1850s).
Carrier to Rye: Catherine Hoad (1850s).
Carrier, *Town & Country Carriers*: Bridget Barton, 7 East St. (1853, 1861).

Chair maker, Maria Shoesmith. 13 All Saints' Street.
Chair bottomer, Ann Quinnal, 96 All Saints' Street (1861).

Eating- and coffee-house keepers:

Mrs. Ann Hyland, 29 George Street (1839, 1845).

Mrs. Eliza Stewart, 29 George Street (1859).

Mrs Reed, Fishmarket.

Mrs Ramsay, Russell Street.

Mary Monk, 20 Havelock Road.

Coffee house, Mary Church, 2 London Road St Leonards.

Coffee house, Sarah Bollinbroke, Russell Street (1841).

Fly Proprietor, Mrs. Mary Glyde, 4 Hill Street (bankrupt 1866).

Hairdresser, Frances Shirley, 40 George Street (1841).

Hairdresser, wigmaker, and perfumer Mrs. Russell (1864).

Ironers:

Jane Cramp, 143 All Saints' Street.

Elizabeth Heayott, Shepherd Street (1841).

Elizabeth Jackson, 5 Stonefield Road.

Margaret Philcox, 4 Russell Street.

Elizabeth Tapp, 1 North Street.

Sarah Bloom, 11½ Bourne Street. (1861).

Laundresses - omitted, as they were far too numerous to list.

Library & Reading Room, Sarah Austin, Marine Parade 1824.

Mangle-women:

Elizabeth Reed, 9 West Street.

Caroline Swaine, rear of 111 All Saints' Street (1861).

Elizabeth Page, 1 Bourne Road.

Sarah White, 12 John Street.

Nurses:

Nurse, East Sussex Infirmary, White Rock. Mrs. Lucy Squires (1850s).

Hannah Bennett, Wellington Mews (1841).

Martha Mitchell, London Road (monthly nurse) (1841).

Mary Farcey, Shepherd Street (1841).

Martha Fernor, London Road, (1841).

Ann Davis, 96 All Saints' Street.

Ann Stone, 14 Stone Street.

Sarah Jennings, 114 All Saints' Street.

Susannah Scott, Gensing Road.

Amelia Roff, 16 Stone Street.

Catherine Gallop & Rhoda Blanchard, 2 Cambridge Terrace.

Eliza Peters, 6 Wellington Terrace.

Anna Walker, 115 High Street.

Mary Waters, 138 All Saints' Street.

Mary Fuller, 110 All Saints' Street.

Jane Padgham, Long House.

Ann Phillips, Adams Cottage.

Ellen Phillips, Heath Cottage.

Matilda Standen, 39, All Saints' Street.

Janet Weeks, London Road, Ore.

Pawnbroker, Sarah Betts, 36 Bourne Street. (1849).

Plumber, glazier & painter, Mrs. Mary Hall, 19 East Ascent.

Printer, Mrs. Charlotte Osborne, 55 George Street.

PRIVATE SCHOOL PROPRIETORS AND PRIVATE TUTORS, 1817-1854

Private schools, academies and seminaries 1817-1841

Boarding school, 2 Burdett Place, Mary Todhunter (1832).
Boarding School. Mrs Mary Kelly, High Street (1824).
Boarding school, Mrs. Goddard, High Street (1826-28).
Ladies' Seminary. Mrs. Charlotte Richards, All Saints' Street (1824-28).
Boarding School, 1 Blucher Buildings, Sarah Bray (1824-32).
Mrs. Edgar, 53 Marina (1833).
Mrs. Ranger, Double-West Villa (1833).
Mrs. Wood, East Ascent (1833).
Sophia Gidds (1840).
Private School at 115-6 High Street, Misses Clarke (1839).
Private School at 81 High Street, Miss Jackson & Miss Dunk (1840).
Private School at 55 Marina, Ann Edgar.
Children's Day School, Mrs. Sarah Stanbridge, All Saints' Street.

Seminaries

Misses Eliza, Margaret & Jane Twiddy, 81 High Street.
Mrs. And Miss Blogg, 115 High Street.
Miss Dunk, Castle Hill.
Miss Whistler, High Street.
Mrs. Winter, 10 West Hill Cottages.
West Hill Preparatory, Laura Phillips.
Boarding School, 2 Wellington Sq, Sarah Bray.
Fairlight Downs Boarding & Day School, Sophia Adds (or Apps).
Fairlight Downs Day School, Rebecca White.
Preparatory School for Gents, Miss Lydia Borrow, 117 High Street.

Private Schools, 1841-1870.

Ladies' Boarding School, 4 High Street, Matilda Hodder.
Boarding School, 118 Marina, Eliza Kempson.
Boarding & Day School, 5 Coburg Place, Caroline Matilda Hatton.
Day School, 20 St Andrews Terrace, Catherine Ann Foster.
Seminary, Coburg Place, Mrs. Joseph Samson.
Seminary, Holloway House, Maria Rich.
Seminary, West Hill Cottage, Mrs. Charlotte Vidler.
Seminary, 6 Havelock Road, Mrs. Ellen Champion.
Seminary, 78 High Street, Jane & Eleanor Pink.
Ladies' School, 4 Wellington Terrace, Ellen Rosina Russell.
School proprietresses, Prospect House, Ore. Sarah & Sophia Ades.
London Road. Preparatory School mistress, Emma Davis.
Boarding Seminary 53 Marina., Misses A., E., and F. Edgar.
Preparatory School mistress, 22 East Ascent, Miss Mary Reed.
Ladies' Seminary, 1 Albion Cottages, Miss Mary Ann Lancaster.
Ladies' School, 2 Albion Cottages, Lucy Clarke, teacher of French, Music and Drawing.
Ladies' School, 41 All Saints' Street, Mrs. Ginner.
Ladies' School, Waterloo Place, Mrs. Elizabeth Wise.
Ladies' School, Waterloo Place, Miss Ann. F Wise, Music Teacher.
Ladies' School, Hill Street, The Misses Wise.

Ladies' School, 12 London Road, Frances Wise.

Ladies' School, 1 Trinity Street Miss Jordan (1867).

Ladies' Seminary, Sarah Elizabeth Gates, Portland Cottage.

Boarding School, 1 Castledown Terrace, Miss Caroline Nichols, (head).[17]

Boarding School, 6 Castledown Terrace, Catherine Freer.

Boarding School, 35 Wellington Sq, Miss Fanny and Miss Magdaline Clifton.

Boarding School, 27 Wellington Sq, Mrs. Emily D' Oyly.

Ladies' Boarding School, Halloway Place, Misses Chapman and Bonnick.

Ladies' School, 1 Croft Place, Miss Peach.

Ladies' school, 18 St. Mary's Terrace. Mrs. J Jennings (1864).

Day School, Russell Cottage, East Hill, Charlotte Smith.

Day School, Wood's Passage, Charlotte Smith. (1862).

Girls' Private Boarding School. 8 East Parade, Miss J.N. Thompson, Teacher of Music & Languages. In partnership with Ellen Kidd.

Boy's School, 64 St Mary's Terrace. Matron, Ann Hubert (1861).

Boy's School, 62 St Mary's Terrace. Proprietor, Elizabeth Cullum(1861).

Boy's School, 62 St Mary's Terrace. Music teacher, Sarah Norwood (1861).

Boys' prep. school, 4 Priory Garden Villas, Bohemia Road, Miss Moor, Mrs. Lamb.

Boys' School, 6 Archery Villas, Miss Henrietta Pennington.

Boys' prep. School, 5 Maze Hill, Elizabeth & Matilda Austin.

Boys' prep. School, 7 Cavendish Terrace, Mrs. Caroline Simes.

Ladies College, 7 Castledown Terrace. Principal, Catherine Farr.

Boarding School, Miss Andrews, 3 High Street (1867).

Private Tutors

Frau Winkelman, Professor of German, 23 London Road.

Miss Bacon, Professor of Singing and Music, 9 Claremont.

Mrs. Hannah Begbie, Professor of Singing and Music, 14 Russell Street.

Miss Pinter, Professor of Music 102 Marina.

Mrs. Sophia Alvey, Teacher of Music, 62 St Mary's Terrace.

Miss Mary Hough, Drawing Teacher, 2 Paragon Bldgs.

Mrs. Louisa Rising, Professor of Music, South Lodge West.

Mariana Fisher, drawing teacher, 4 Prospect Place.

Julia Charpentier, Teacher of French, 2 Trinity Street.

Maria Murray, Linguist and Professor of Music, 4 Trinity Street.

Caroline Hugeman, Professor of Languages, 10 High Street (1861).

Martha Poster, Professor of Music. 7 Wellington Place.

Mademoiselle Tonge, teacher of French and German. (1864).

WOMEN EMPLOYED BY CHURCHES, HOSPITALS AND CHARITIES.

Chapel Keeper, Lucy Smith, Congregational Chapel, Robertson Street (1861).
Lady Superintendent, Ladies' Home, Catherine House, Church Rd. Miss Cooper (1870).
Manager, Albert House Ladies' Home & Soup Kitchen, Cross St: Emma Baker (1870).
Manager, St Mary's Convalescent Home for Women, 80 High St. Lydia Clark (1870).
Manageress, St Mary's soup-kitchen, Wellington Terrace: Louisa Goodwin (1870).
Matron of Servants' Home, 5 Western Road, St. L: Mrs. Ann Callan (1870).
Matron, Children's Convalescent Home, Stanhope Place. Mrs. Hulbert (1870).
Matron, East Sussex Infirmary, White Rock. Frances Cable Hartley.
Matron, Infirmary, White Rock. Mary Ann Griffin (1861).
Matron, St Clement's Workhouse: Miss Judith White (1835) (later Mrs. Harman).
Matron, Hastings Union Workhouse: Mrs. Judith Harman (1850s).
Matron, Hastings Union Workhouse: Mrs. Monk (1870).
Matron, Bourne Street Gaol. Mary Wellerd (died 1846).
Matron, Bourne Street Gaol. Ann Wellerd (1848).
Matron, Bourne Street Gaol. Amelia Wellerd (1846-8).
Matron, St Mary's Poorhouse, Hannah Goodwin (1828-37).
Matron, Mendicity House, Bourne Passage: Mrs. Elizabeth Bentley (1859).
Matron, West Hill Industrial School: Mrs. Maria Marshall (1850s).
Mistress, School of Industry, Albion Place: Miss Marshall. (1870).[18]
Pew openers, All Saints' Church, 1850s.
    Jane Bafford, 1 Burdett Place.
    Mrs. Bailey, 2 Church Yard (until 1848).
    Mrs. Hannah Goodwin, 2 Church Yard (1848-1854).
    Pew Opener, Oare (sic) Church Mrs. Giles. (1835).
    Pew Opener, Croft Chapel. Frances Boreham. (1862).
Principal, Children's Convalescent Home, Stanhope Place. Miss Giesler (1870).
Superintendent, Industrial Kitchen & Ladies' Home, Mrs. Eccardt.
Superintendent, Invalids' Kitchen, Albert House, Cross St: Emma Baker (1861).

REFERENCES

[1] An Elizabeth Sargent had been licensee of the Hastings Arms 1798-99.
[2] Also proprietress of the Warm Baths.
[3] The 1841 Census shows the licensee as John Tritton, married to Frances, with four children.
[4] Applied for full license and became a public-house.
[5] Joint business with younger brother, By 1867 they were also selling sea weeds, cutlery, combs, shell work and perfumes.
[6] Mary had this shop for about 15 years. It was a joint business with her husband, a cobbler.
[7] Husband a fisherman, eight children aged 2 to 17.
[8] Married to a whitesmith, 5 children.
[9] Her husband was a shrimper.
[10] Born in Paris in 1803, she was married to an out-of-work tradesman and had 4 daughters.
[11] With her sister Ann, also ran a lodging house above the shop.
[12] Employed a boy of 12. Prosecuted him in 1855 for stealing 5s for till. She begged leniency. He received 7 days in Lewes House of Correction.
[13] Presumably, a stockist of children's clothing.
[14] She also ran a servant's registry office at 1 Carlisle Parade the at 19 London Road. (1867).
[15] b.1804, married to a tailor, three children.
[16] Also kept lodging houses and a Theological Library.
[17] Run with her cousin Jane. They had 8 pupils and 3 female servants.
[18] She was Matron for 22 years until her death in 1871.

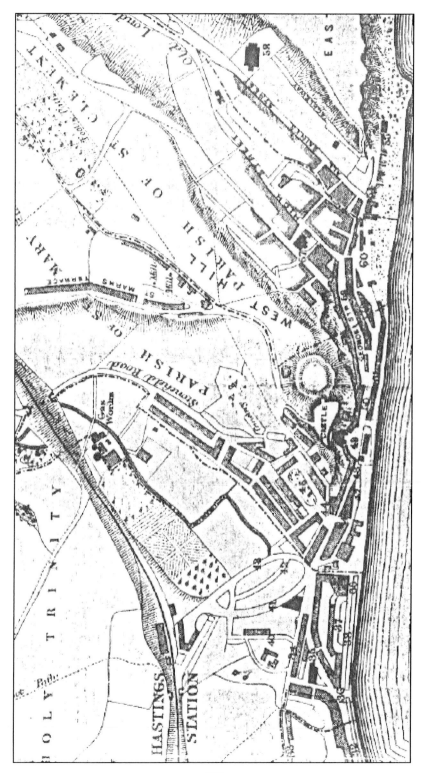

Gant's map of Hastings, 1855.

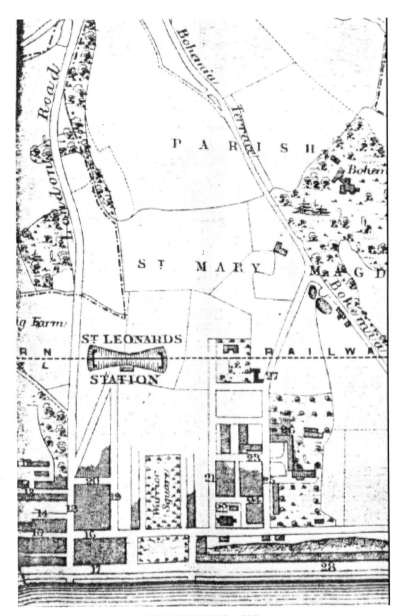

ST LEONARDS, 1855.
Showing Warrior Square, the station, London Road and Bohemia Terrace.

12 - Alfred Street. 13 - North Street. 14 - Shepherd Street.
15 - Norman Road West. 16- Norman Road East. 17 - Grand Parade.
18 - London Road. 19 - Western Road. 20 - Cross Street.
21 - Church Road. 22 - St Mary Magdalen Church. 23. Victoria Street.
24 - St Mary's Place. 25 - Magdalen Road. 26 - Convent of All Souls.
27 - National Schools. 28 - Eversfield Place.

160

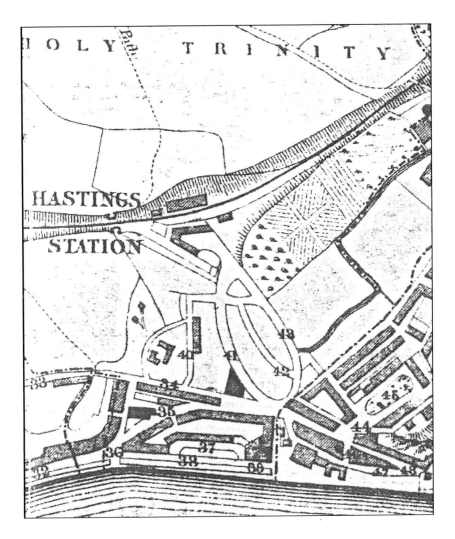

WEST-CENTRAL HASTINGS, 1855.

29 -Verulam Place. 30 - Infirmary. 31- White Rock Villa. 32 - White Rock
Place. 33 - Trinity Terrace. 34 - Linton Terrace (now Cambridge Rd).
35 - Holy Trinity Church. 36 - Robertson Street. 37 - Robertson Terrace.
38 - Carlisle Parade. 40 - Priory Street. 41- Havelock Road.

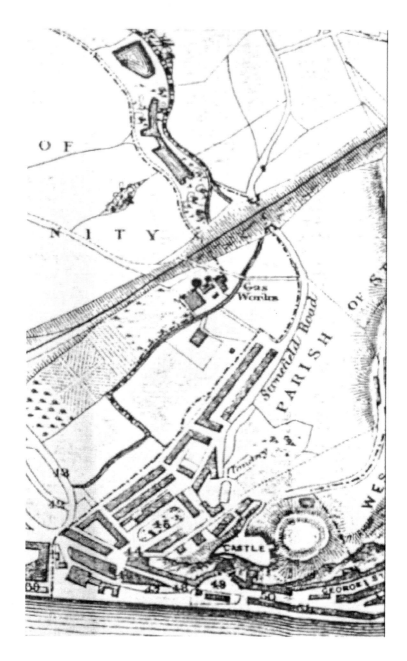

EAST-CENTRAL HASTINGS, 1855.

Showing the railway line, Castle, and empty fields north of Meadow Road (now
Queen's Road), which is marked by the broken line.
Safeway now covers the gasworks site.
39 - Queen's Hotel. 42 - Middle Street. 43 - Station Road. 44 - Wellington Place. 46
- Wellington Square. 47 - Caroline Place. 48 - Breeds Place.
49 - Pelham Crescent. 50 - Pelham Place.

EAST HASTINGS, THE OLD TOWN, 1855.
Showing the two railway tunnels, High St, All Saints' St and Tackleway.
55 - Fishermen's Church. 57 - St Clement's Church.
58 - All Saints' Church. 60 - Fish Market, 68 George Street.

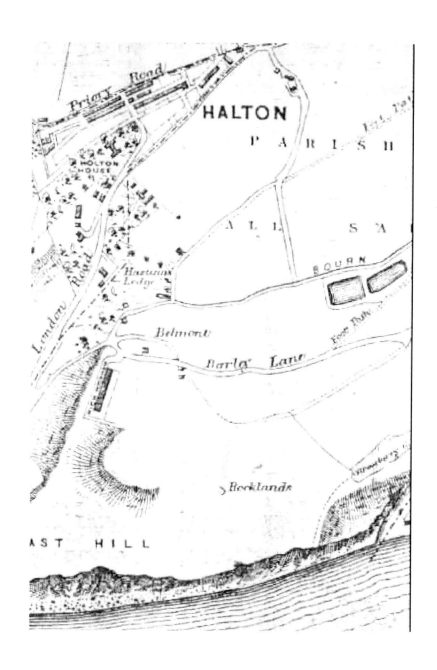

EAST OF HASTINGS, 1855.
Showing the MP's house Hastings Lodge, and Rocklands Farm

Laing's map of Hastings, 1859.

Map of Hastings, 1859
Section 1: west Hastings. Trinity Terrace is now Cambridge Road.

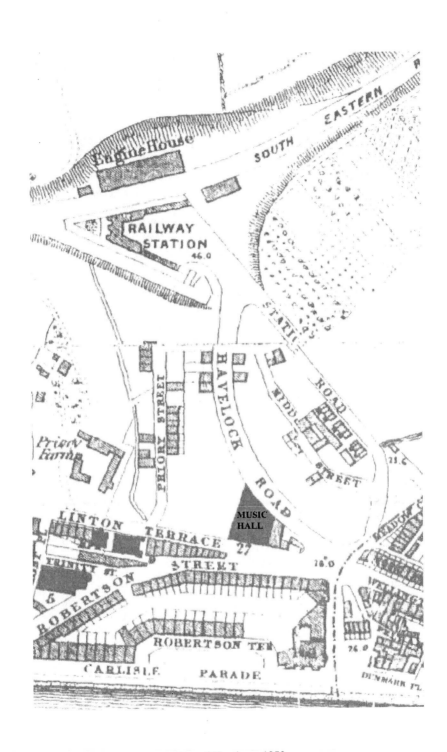

Map of Hastings, 1859
Section 2: central Hastings. Linton Terrace is now Cambridge Road.

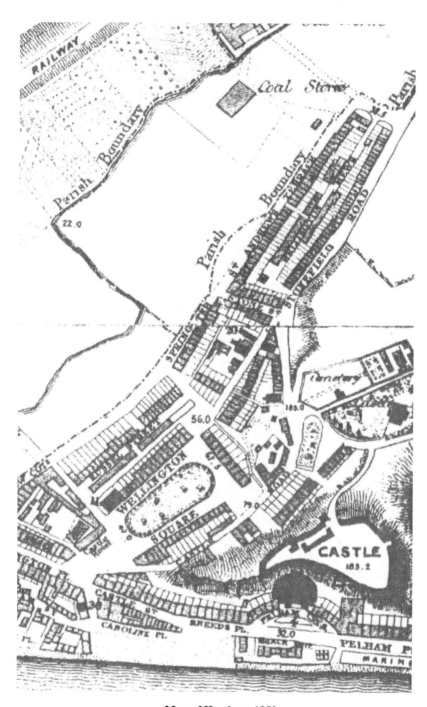

Map of Hastings, 1859
Section 3: east-central Hastings.
The large building at the eastern end of Pelham Crescent beneath the word 'castle' is
Pelham Baths. Spring Terrace and St Andrews Terrace are now Queen's Road.

168

MID-VICTORIAN PRICES & WAGES

d = pennies.   s = shillings.   12d = 1s.   20s = £1.

Average Prices in 1850

Beef pound	8d
Cheese, pound	7d
Butter, pound	1s 1d
Eggs (12) summer	1s 10d
Eggs, (12) winter	11d
Rent of room in house, weekly	3s 0d
Rent of cottage, weekly	5s 0d
Bed & board & laundry, weekly	8s 6d
Rent of small house, weekly	6s 0d
Rent of 12-bed house, Marina, weekly	65s 0d
Rent, 20-1 High St. (21 rooms) weekly	19s 0d
Excursion train fare to London, return, (1859) 3rd class covered carriage	3s 6d
2nd class	5s 6d
1st Class	7s 6d
Usual return fare to London 3rd class	9s 9d
16 year lease for shop and five rooms in Norman Rd	£680.00
Weekly rent of same	9s 0d
Guinness, pint	3s 6d
Photo taken in Pelham Arcade	1s 0d
Childminder, weekly	5s 0d

Average weekly wages 1850s

Pew opener, female	7d
Schoolmistress	7s 6d
Domestic servant	4s 0d
Cook	5s 0d
Skilled tradeswoman	20s 0d
Skilled tradesman	30s 0d
National Schoolmistress	7s 0d
National Schoolmaster	23s 0d
Borough Treasurer, male	27s 0d
Superintendent of Police	61s 0d

NB: Domestic servants also received bed and board, and schoolmasters and mistresses a rent-free house, as part of their remuneration.

AMUSING SIMPLICITY.—Some days ago, a young woman, too obviously "from the country," was seen standing with a very perplexed air at one of the pillar letter-boxes. She was observed to knock several times on the top of the iron pillar, but obtaining no response she passed round to the opposite side, and raising the cover of the slit in which letters are placed, she applied her mouth to the aperture, and called out, loud enough for the amazed bystanders to hear, "Can you let me have a postage stamp?"

Miscellaneous Milestones

For women and for Hastings
1829-1872

1829   First child born in St Leonards, on 6 April - Emma Martha Mawle.

1829   The Philpot sisters open the first business in Marina Colonnade.

1830   Gas works established on site of Old Priory Mill – now Safeway's.

1830   Sophia Jex-Blake born at Croft Road.

1831   Town gas-lit for the first time.

1832   First Reform Bill extended the vote to men who owned or rented property worth an annual rate of £10 or more (about 18% of the adult male population). It introduced the word 'male' into suffrage legislation for the first time.

1831   Public water first supplied to both towns.

1834   Visit of Princess Victoria and her mother the Duchess of Kent.

1836   First police officers in Hastings.

1837   Visit of the Dowager Queen Adelaide.

1839   Infants and Child Custody Act allowed women who were divorced or separated but had not been proved adulterous to ask for custody of children under seven. Custody of those over seven always went automatically to the father.

1840   Marianne North born at Hastings Lodge.

1841   First hospital, in High Street.

        Board of Health finds one-third of Old Town homes unsanitary.

1852   First female passenger to be killed while travelling by rail from St Leonards. Schoolmistress Mrs Edwards, aged 67, from Norman Road, fell out of an open carriage and was found lying by the side of the track west of Bexhill. She later died of her injuries.

1857   Hastings Cottage Improvement Society founded.

        Matrimonial Causes Act/Divorce Act established secular divorce in England. Prior to this divorce required an act of Parliament and cost hundreds of pounds, and only four women had ever achieved a divorce this way. The 1857 law provided that (1) a court could order maintenance payment to a divorced or estranged wife; (2) a divorced wife could inherit or bequeath property, enter contracts, sue or be sued, and protect her earnings from a deserter; (3) a man could secure a divorce on the grounds of his wife's adultery. For women, a husband's adultery alone was insufficient grounds.

1861   Volunteer Fire Brigade founded.

1863   Queen's Hotel opened.

1864   Cricket ground opened on site of Priory Meadow.

1867   Second Reform Bill doubled the electorate by extending the vote to almost all working men except agricultural day-labourers. An amendment by John Stuart Mill to include women was overwhelmingly defeated.

Amendment to the Municipal Franchise Act* enabled women ratepayers to vote for local municipal councils (see 1872). Women form up to a fifth of the municipal electorate.

1869   Women allowed to stand for Poor Law Boards, and thus become Poor Law Guardians.

1870   Education Act. Compulsory, free education for all children.

1870   Elementary Education Act allowed all qualified rate paying women to vote for members of School Boards, and any woman to stand.

Married Women's Property Act mandated that women could keep their earnings and inherit personal property and small amounts of money; everything else (whether acquired before or after marriage) belonged to their husbands.

1872   Municipal Franchise Act (see * above) Married women now excluded from voting in local municipal elections.

New Custody Act: divorcing women could be awarded custody of children under the age of 16.

FURTHER READING

Women's history:

Alexander, Sally, *Women workers in Victorian London,* in: Mitchell, J. and Oakley, A. *Rights and wrongs of women*. Penguin, 1976.

Burman, Sandra, *Fit work for women* Croom Helm, 1979.

Clark, A, *Working life of women in the 17th century*. Routledge & Kegan Paul 1982

Hilery, M, *Victorian working women: portraits from life*. Gordon Fraser Gallery, 1979.

Pennington, Shelley and Westover, Belinda, *A hidden workforce: home workers in England 1850-1985*. Macmillan, 1989.

Pinchbeck, Ivy, *Women workers and the industrial revolution*. Virago, 1981

Purvis, J, *Women's History; Britain, 1850-1945*.

Roberts, Elizabeth, *Women's work 1840-1940*. Macmillan, 1988.

Taylor, B, '*The men are as bad as their masters..':socialism, feminism, and sexual antagonism in the London tailoring trade in the early 1830s*. (Feminist Studies; v.6 no.1, 1979)

Tilly, L. and Scott, J.W. *Women, work and family*. Methuen, 1987.

Vicinus, M, (Ed.) *Suffer and be Still: Women in the Victorian Age*. Methuen, 1980.

Walkley, C, *The ghost in the looking glass: The Victorian seamstress*. Peter Owen, 1981

Hastings History:

Brett, T. B. *Histories* and *Historico-Biographies*, unpublished, held at Hastings Library.

Elleray, Robert, *Hastings: A pictorial history*. Phillimore, 1979.

Haines, Gavin, *Britain in old photographs: Hastings & St Leonards*, Alan Sutton 1997.

Haines, Pamela, *Hastings in old photographs*. Alan Sutton, 1989.

Hastings Local History Group, *Hastings Bygones* Volumes 1, 2, 3, & 4.

Hastings Modern History Workshop, *Priory Meadow & the Town Centre*. 1997.

Manwaring Baines, J. *Historic Hastings*. Parsons, 1955.

Marchant, R. *Hastings Past*. Phillimore, 1997.

Meredith, James, *Old Town Hastings*, Meredith Press 1986.

Scott, A, *Hastings in old picture postcards*. European Library, Netherlands, 1993.

Thornton, David, *Hastings: A living history*. David Thornton, 1987.

Wales, T, *The Archive Photographs Series: Hastings*. Chalford, 1998.

INDEX

STAYS! STAYS!! STAYS!!!

The doctors say, "Don't take
    to wearing stays."
The ladies say, "We'll have
    our own ways."
P'rhaps, after all, the ladies'
    plan is best;
If so, 'tis clear the question's
    set at rest.
But whether wearing stays be
    good or bad,
I'll tell you where the cheap-
    est may be had.—
Not merely cheap because
    they're low in price,
But more becaus they're really good and nice.

In Norman road, at number 28,
Go! make your purchase, ere you be too late;
For sure am I, the stays of T. B. Brett,
Are cheap beyond all others you can get.

No matter whether grey or drab or white,
They're strongly made, and shape and texture right.
Then go and take your ready-money there,
And buy good stays at SIXTEEN-PENCE a pair.

MUSIC HALL, HASTINGS.

MISS FANNY PITT'S

COMEDY & BURLESQUE COMPANY,

SATURDAY, (THIS DAY) 27th January, 1872,
*GRAND ILLUMINATED MORNING PER-
FORMANCE,*

When will be performed Falconer's Comedy
EXTREMES !

The Performance in the Evening will commence with
the popular serio-comic Drama
"THE FACTORY GIRL,"
And conclude with
ORPHEUS AND EURYDICE.

Directress : MRS. CHARLES PITT

(Late Lessee of the Theatres Royal, Sheffield, Edinburgh, Swansea, Cambridge, and Surrey Theatre.

Doors open at Seven, Performance to commence
at half-past. Tickets to be had at Lockey's Music
Saloon, where a plan of the Room may be seen and
Seats secured.